To S

Love from Katrine

Christmas 1996.

IN THE TROUBLESOME TIMES

Cambo today showing the pele tower on the right and, opposite, the old schoolhouse, altered and enlarged to a hall and reading room in 1911.

IN THE

TROUBLESOME TIMES

Memories of Old Northumberland
Collected by the Cambo Women's Institute

Edited by
Rosalie E. Bosanquet

THE SPREDDEN PRESS
STOCKSFIELD
1989

First published by Northumberland Press Ltd 1929.
Reprinted 1929.

Reprinted, 1989, with new preface,
by The Spredden Press,
Brocksbushes Farm, Stocksfield, Northumberland NE45 7WB

Preface © The Spredden Press

ISBN Hardback   1 871739 02 0
        Paperback   1 871739 03 9

Printed and bound by
SMITH SETTLE
Ilkley Road, Otley, West Yorkshire LS21 3JP

PREFACE TO SECOND EDITION

In the Troublesome Times was first published in 1929 and was reprinted in the same year. In 1922, when the newly formed Women's Institute of Cambo entered the competition described by Rosalie Bosanquet in her Preface, many of the older villagers could remember a childhood in the mid-nineteenth century and a way of life, with its festivals, fairs, fairies and boggles, its songs, dances and handicrafts that had not changed for many centuries. Though some of the customs and traditions described are peculiar to Northumberland most belong to the rural countryside of England that was changed irrevocably by the 1914 war. The 'innumerable talks by firesides' transcribed here by Rosalie Bosanquet, are a precious record of oral history at a time when this was not the easy task that tape recorders have made it today.

The district of the Cambo Women's Institute had a population of 463 in 1911 and it is not much larger today. John Hodgson, whose *History of Northumberland* is quoted frequently here in the section on monuments and place names, described Cambo in 1827 as an 'ancient village situated on the high roads from Hexham to Alnwick, and from Newcastle to Edinburgh, by Jedburgh . . . it consists of a good inn, a pele tower, a school house, and some well-built houses for the agents, and cottages for the mechanics and labourers employed upon the Wallington estate'.

In 1922 a Mrs Haldane, who had been born in the village in 1825, was still alive. She remembered, as a small child would, a 'charming shop where one bought whips and patches for dolls' dresses'. There must have been many shops at that date: a poem of 1842, quoted here, mentions a blacksmith, saddler, butcher, 'clogger', cooper, grocer, shoemaker, joiner and tailor. There was certainly a baker and at that time the local doctor lived in Cambo. There had long been a village school: it had been attended, a century earlier, by Cambo's most famous son, Capability Brown.

Edward Keith, in his privately published *Memories of Wallington* (1939), gives an excellent picture of Sir Charles Edward Trevelyan's improvements in Cambo in the 1880s: 'The village smithy with its wide southern approach open to the highway was turned right face about; its hooping apparatus, its heaps of scrap-iron and discarded farm implements (the refuse of many a bankrupt's sale) were cleared away and the ramshackle hemmels wherein Sir Walter Trevelyan's prize Kyloes were sheltered in the winter months before being sent on to the Birmingham and Smithfield shows pulled down to make way for the walled-in garden and its clanking wicket . . . In the centre of the village the untidy open space whereon had stood for generations the joiner's and cooper's shops and the byres and haystacks of the crofters was cleared, new outhouses and stables erected and the square enclosed by a stone wall, with the intention of making a small public park.'

A Mr James Wilkinson of Hartington, quoted here, remembers that 'there were middens in front of the houses at Cambo but Sir Charles wouldn't have it and made the gardens'. By 1889 Cambo was 'an exceedingly picturesque village . . . with several pretty dwelling houses and cottages, with gardens in front, the whole forming a picture of rustic peace and beauty not easily surpassed in the county' (W. W. Tomlinson, *A Comprehensive Guide to Northumberland*).

What were the troublesome times? There were 'a tremendous long time ago', the time when the Scots came and 'as they travelled they burned'. But the memory's links to the past can be surprisingly long: Sir George Otto Trevelyan (who died in 1928) remembers that his grandfather, when he first came to Wallington, used to talk to a man who remembered the troopers riding down Cambo bank, on their way back from Culloden in 1745. Mrs Haldane recalls 'the coach that brought the news of the passing of the Reform Bill in 1832 and how her father brought all of the household out into the road so that they would be the first to hear the news'. Mrs Pearson's father-in-law fought in the Peninsular War and was a model for one of the canvases painted by William Bell Scott at Wallington. Mrs Hepple had three uncles who fought at Waterloo.

But most of the memories are domestic: the houses people lived in, often with 'no ovens and no windows', the beds they slept in, the school and schoolmasters, the traditional remedies when one was ill and how the great events of life — birth, marriage, death — and the festivals of the year were celebrated. If there are rough edges and some repetition these, as Rosalie Bosanquet says, 'form part of the charm'.

Gillian Dickinson, 1989

Rosalie Ellison Bosanquet, the editor of *In the Troublesome Times*, spent most of her life in Northumberland. Her family and friends knew her as Rose, but she always signed herself Rosalie E. Bosanquet. The family home was Rock Hall about twenty miles to the north east of Cambo. The Bosanquets had owned the house and five farms since 1804, and successive generations combined supervision of the estate with academic and intellectual activities.

Rose's grandfather was parson, as well as squire. Her father qualified as a barrister, and worked for the Charity Organization Society in London before settling down at Rock Hall to raise his large family. Rose was the youngest of eight children. Five daughters came first, followed by two sons. The oldest of these, Robert Carr Bosanquet, was sent to Eton and Trinity College, Cambridge, and was very conscious of the limited education his elder sisters had received from governesses. It was due to his insistence that Rose in her turn was better taught and went to Lady Margaret Hall at Oxford, with a scholarship, taking a first class honours degree in modern history in 1902. She spent the next twelve years doing social work in London and became a Tutor in Social Sciences at the London School of Economics. On the outbreak of war in 1914 Rose returned to Northumberland and for the next four years worked in the vegetable garden at Craster Tower, four miles from Rock, becoming a member of the Women's Land Army.

After the war, Rose went to live at Cambo with her cousin and contemporary, Jessie Carr. She looked after their garden while Jessie ran the house and drove their car. Their house is mentioned several times in this book, notably on pp. 55-6 when its past history as an Inn is recounted. It stood on one of the main roads across the Border and the sign showed the traveller from each direction his own Queen. The name 'The Two Queens' lived on when it became a private house and the sign still hung, but indoors, in a large upper room.

The local Women's Institute became an important part of Rose's life and after two-and-a-half years in the village she was asked to take charge of their collection of local traditions. The book was put into its present form and published seven years later.

Rose and Jessie continued to be active members of the Women's Institute when they moved to a farmhouse on the Rock estate. It was known as Rock South Farm but Rose, typically, preferred to use the older name of Gull Ha' (the northern version of Hall). Rock Hall, her old home, was not let and has since become a Youth Hostel. Her brother, and later her nephew, lived at Rock Moor, another enlarged farmhouse. Robert Carr Bosanquet and his wife are mentioned among those who helped her with this book. He had been Director of the British School of Archaeology at Athens, and a Professor of Liverpool University before settling at Rock. His eldest son later became Vice Chancellor of Newcastle University.

Before the outbreak of war in 1939 Rose had left Northumberland. Jessie had died and she was anxious to be near her sisters in the south, one of whom had recently returned from a lifetime working for the Church Missionary Society in Tokyo. Rose never again had a settled home of her own but lived in guest houses and visited relations. She died on 10 October 1957 in a nursing home in Henley on Thames.

PREFACE TO THE SECOND EDITION

This book is the fruit of the happiest time of her life, when she was an active member of a lively village community. She was a gentle, diffident person; otherwise she might have edited the contributions more severely and cut out some repetition. But she was very much aware of the personalities behind each anecdote and memory and of the disappointment that might result from such pruning.

Rosemary Goyder, 1989

PREFACE

In October, 1921, a prize was offered by Miss Grace Hadow in the pages of " Home and Country, the·Women's Institute Journal," for the best book compiled by a Women's Institute on old Customs, Beliefs, Stories, and Ancient Monuments, etc.

Members of the Cambo W.I. became aware of this in January, 1922, and recalling the tales of the Elves' Track and of the Warlock told by old residents, they quickly decided that Cambo should compete.

By the end of September, the following materials had been hastily gathered and thrown together,—largely thanks to opportune snowstorms. There were innumerable talks by firesides,—the mothers and grandmothers and, the menfolk opening the treasures of their memories, with the younger women joining in the discussion. There were talks— " cracks " as we call them—walking along snowy roads. We admitted men to our " Folk-Lore Evenings." One father even interrupted his shaving to dash out and tell us a story. There were days when members and their relatives took us newcomers to see old houses, " camps " and pre-historic remains. We were helped by a " Treasure Evening " when we showed each other our old treasures. Unavoidably, owing to lack of time, the picture drawn is impressionist, but it is perhaps all the more true for that reason.

The Prize of £5 was awarded to Fenstanton W.I. in Huntingdonshire for a scholarly book prepared by Miss Peet.[1] The judge, Dr. Marett, had had difficulty in making the award and Miss Hadow kindly gave a special prize of £2 2s. to Cambo. Five short extracts appeared in " Home and Country."

Besides our contributors, and besides those whom we have mentioned in the following letter to Miss Hadow, we owe thanks to so many friends that we scarcely dare begin to name them.

[1] See Appendix A.

5

Miss Grace Hadow and Dr. Marett gave us the idea. Dr. H. H. E. Craster, Mr. Henry Richardson, Professor Lethaby, Mrs. Nugent Harris, the late Dr. Bernard Bosanquet, Mr. and Mrs. R. C. Bosanquet, Mr. D. D. Dixon, the late Mr. Howard Pease, the Rev. R. R. Hedley and Mrs. Hedley, the Rev. R. B. Dawson, Mrs. Alfred Finch, Miss Elinor Middleton, Dr. Dendy, Mr. R. Cecil Hedley, Mr. W. P. Hedley and Mrs. G. M. Trevelyan have each given a strengthening hand, and some of them have helped us over obstacles that had seemed insurmountable.

Some of our own members have done more than would be supposed from the one or two mentions of them. Miss Mitchell and the late Mrs. Rutherford, the one from Scotland, the other from County Durham, valued our folk-lore and helped on the scheme. Lady Trevelyan, Miss McCracken, the late Miss Brown of Newbiggin, Miss Charlton, Miss Hilda Hedley and others have read through parts or the whole, and have given advice.

Mr. Edward Keith had the kindness to go through the manuscript and has made additions. We are sure that Miss Nellie Brown and other Institute members suggested sayings about the weather, luck, etc., which, for lack of a shorthand writer, have not been credited to them.

The heart of the book was written in 1922. It was impossible to get it published then in spite of the number of people who wished to read it; since then deaths, marriages, changes of name, age, work and address have taken place. We cannot bring it up to date. As a picture of ourselves in 1922 we are all alive at Cambo and talking together; in 1929 we should be a broken circle; for me as I read it, all the old folk are here, the present Sir Charles and Lady Trevelyan are Mr. and Mrs. Trevelyan, Mrs. Stevenson is Miss Barbara Blain, Miss Richardson is schoolmistress. The list of contributors shows which of them have left this world, or have married; changes of address and of work we cannot attempt to give. Two or three wise friends have implored me not to try to make improvements,—" the rough edges and the unexpectedness form part of the charm."

R.E.B.

Cambo,
    June, 1929.

CONTENTS

7

8 CONTENTS

PART III
STORIES AND MUSIC

PART IV
ANCIENT MONUMENTS AND PLACE NAMES

INTRODUCTORY NOTE

September, 1922.

DEAR MISS HADOW,

We have to thank you for some interesting months in the past, and perhaps in the future too, for this subject has aroused such interest that members are saying " Is it going to be printed? " It is not yet a book, it is only notes for a book, and we apologize for sending it in so rough a form, but material has come in overwhelmingly fast at the last.

We have had two Institute Meetings devoted wholly to the discussion of old days, and half an Institute Committee. All the sixteen officers and members of Committee have contributed, and more than half the ordinary members. Our President, Mrs. Charles Trevelyan, has been entirely responsible for music and dance, with help from Miss Truelove in writing down music.

Miss J. D. Carr has been practically assistant editor, lending her ears, her memory, and advice, and she did her best to take the place of a shorthand writer.

Our members' relations, friends, and neighbours have thrown themselves into our interest most enthusiastically, and the members have referred us to the best authorities on all subjects.

Thanks to the kindness of Mrs. Straker and Mrs. Bell we have been introduced to valuable authorities in Mr. Perceval and Miss Robson of Angerton in our old mother parish of Hartburn. Except for them and for a few near relations of members we haven't had time to go outside " our district."

Cambo Women's Institute has about eighty members, which it draws from a district roughly coinciding with the ecclesiastical parish of Cambo, but a few members come from beyond—from the group of houses near Middleton Station, and from White Hill near Kirkwhelpington.

Cambo is our only real village, and it numbers twenty-four houses. There are a great number of grass farms, many of which have only one or two houses, so you will understand that we have to refer to a large number of different place names even within our inner circle. When we speak of places beyond this " district " we have tried to make it clear for the sake of the reader at a distance.

The population of the ecclesiastical parish was 463 in 1911, and the acreage is 15,620 acres: the parish is several miles in length and breadth.

We run down to and across the river Wansbeck on the south, and right up to the Rothbury moors to the north.

As to our method of writing the " book," you can guess from the figures just given what a busy community we are, and how little time most of us have for writing. To a great extent I have had to be the pen of the Institute, but the Institute and its friends have guided the pen. I only came to live in this part of Northumberland two and a half years ago,—though Northumbrian born and bred, and it has been a true case of an Institute educating and teaching one of its Vice-Presidents. Even my books of reference have been almost exclusively lent me by the members and their relations. When first the floodgates of memory were opened, even a shorthand writer could not have taken down word for word. We had to commit to memory every word we could, write it down at once at home, and return on a later day with the proofs to be revised by our authority. Later on pencil and paper were in constant use. Nearly every long statement has been discussed with the speaker at least twice, but the responsibility for inaccuracies must rest on my shoulders.

We despaired at first of finding any Customs, or " Beliefs " that were not in books, so we decided to disregard books and write down as complete an account as we could of what we considered our own customs and beliefs; and in doing so we have, we hope, noted some variations at any rate, and perhaps a few that are not in books.

John Hodgson's excellent " History of Northumberland,"— Part II, Vol. I, written when he was Vicar of our neighbouring parish of Kirkwhelpington, and published in 1827, is a mine of information about this part, and so is E. Mackenzie's similar history. We have tried to avoid repeating what they say.

Believe me, yours sincerely,

ROSALIE E. BOSANQUET

(one of the Vice-Presidents of

Cambo Women's Institute)

THE TWO QUEENS,

CAMBO, MORPETH,

NORTHUMBERLAND.

PART I

CUSTOMS

CHAPTER I

CUSTOMS FOR SPECIAL DAYS

First-Footing.

" *A dark man* should be the first one in on New Year's morning; a fair man's unlucky, and a woman's worst of all."

A Meeting of the Women's Institute were unanimous about this, and one member exclaimed, " But a woman never gets the chance ! "

The men, especially the lads, go round first-footing as soon as the clock has struck twelve—from house to house, and from village to farm, with much shouting and musical instruments.

" They're supposed to *fetch in a bit of stick or coal for the fire*. There was one year we had bits all along there "—pointing to the fender.—Mrs. Wilson, blacksmith's wife, Cambo.

" People don't like a woman to be the first one in, and even if it's a man they like him to bring something with him." —Miss Mary Wales, school-teacher.

" Brodie[1] of Broom House used always to be our first-foot, and he used to bring a bit of coal, or a log of wood and *put it on the fire*."—Mrs. Wales, wife of tailor, Cambo.

There is always something on the table, and the first-footers do not go away hungry or thirsty.

Thomas Hepple always would have me come along with the lads, and we used to go there last, and there was always breakfast for us—bacon and eggs.

They made even more of it before the war than they do

---

[1] He was seventy-five when he died in 1921.

now. The lads used to go up the Church Tower and ring the bells. Once the sexton who was here then locked them in; they'd come to help him ring the midnight bell, and they couldn't get out, and he went round the village and did the first-footing himself!

There was one time George Handyside didn't want to get up and let them in, so they piled up all the boxes they could find in front of his door, and he just looked out o' window, and said " Ye've done that gey weel! " [1]

On other occasions the first-footers when not admitted have been known to upset water barrels, to trundle a wheel-barrow away to the roadside, indeed, " the cart of a former Cambo butcher was always out by the roadside on New Year's morning."—Mr. William Wilson, blacksmith, Cambo.

" After first-footing the lads go out and *tie the doors,* so that people can't get out; one back door can often be tied to the back door opposite."—Miss Hilda Hedley, Post Office, Cambo.

Mrs. Keith says that when she was a child at the Dovecot, " the door snecks[2] used to be tied with ropes one to another so the more you tried to open them the tighter they were! "

And it was the same when Mrs. Pearson was a child at Rothley. Mrs. Pearson is seventy-seven.

We have heard of this feature of first-footing as " barring in " in the present day at the fishing village of Craster, thirty or forty miles from here.

" Mr. Forster[3] always used to be our first-foot; he came round in the morning, no, not in the middle of the night. He liked to be, so we never let anybody in till he had been.

" At Cambo they put water-barrels leaning in against the doors, and water in them! "—Mr. and Mrs. James Wilkinson, Hartington.

" At any hour *on New Year morning* it is *customary to offer cake and wine* to any visitor who happens to come in."—Mrs. Keith, wife of head gardener, Wallington.

Mrs. Hepple (widow of the late Thomas Hepple, farmer, Rugley Walls, who died in 1918, aged seventy-six) says, " The

---

[1] " Very well."

[2] Latches.

[3] Mr. Forster died in 1907 at the age of eighty-eight.

first-footers used to come to our house at one and two in the morning,—all the lads, and we were always up, and I always kept the fire on and had tea and coffee for them; I thought it was better for young lads than whisky. I've always made rhubarb wine since I was a girl, and they liked that too. They always brought in *something to burn.* I've known them bring in a post out of the fence rather than nothing. They lost heart and didn't come during the war, but we had three or four again this year."

Mrs. Hepple, who is eighty years of age, has heard it said that it was *unlucky* for a *red-haired man,* a ginger man, to be the first one in, but she will not allow that there is any harm in a fair man. " They just come in here as they like."

What her husband thought more important seems to have been that *every member of the household,* even the bairns, *should bring in three things* with them the first time they came in, and overnight he used to lay ready—coal, stick and sand. These three things must be brought in before you take anything out, or before you even empty the ashes out, and the words with which they are brought in are—" *Here's my sonce, and here's my sele, and here's my happy New Year.*"

Mrs. Hepple, and her sister, Miss Shipley, aged ninety-three, cannot quite say what the meaning is, but the idea is a present, and " sonce " is connected with " soncy "—a " soncy old body is a canny body." (Miss Shipley.) Mrs. Hepple has heard of some people not being soncy—the pitmen if they meet a woman will turn back, she and Miss Shipley have heard. And Mrs. Hepple thinks we shall not be far wrong if we take " sonce " as meaning " luck." But of " sele " they can offer no explanation.[1]

There can be very few, if any, houses in our district where the custom of first-footing is not respected.

Miss Gow says that three things—coal, wood, and cake are brought into her house on New Year's morning. Whisky used to be one of the things but hers is a teetotal house.

She is a daughter of the late Mr. Gow, the agent of the Wallington estate, who came to Cambo in 1847.

---

[1] John Jamieson's " Scottish Dictionary," published 1808, translates Sons, Sonce as prosperity, felicity, abundance; and Seile, Seyle, Sele as happiness, prosperity.

S. Valentine's Day.

Valentines used to be sent, and *gloves given.*—Institute Meeting.

" A great deal was made of it when I was a girl."—Mrs. Hedley, Cambo Post Office.

This used to be a great day, but " less notice has been taken of it since post cards came in." Lots of Valentines were sent, both nice ones and spiteful ones; " if anybody didn't like you, or wanted to huff you " they sent a spiteful Valentine, or an envelope with something written outside for anybody to read, and slipped them under the door.

Shrove Tuesday.

Pancakes are eaten, and always have been eaten here.— Institute Meeting, confirmed by Mrs. Hedley.

The pancake bell is still rung at our market town, Morpeth, twelve miles from here. It is rung from the bell tower in the centre of the town.—Miss Murray, daughter of farmer, Rothley Park Farm.

Football is played at Rothbury, twelve miles from here; the shops are shut up whilst they have a frolic. Apprentices claim a half holiday.—A member at Institute Meeting.

Mothering Sunday. 4th Sunday in Lent.

The girls come home, not the boys.—Mrs. Keith.

Carlin Sunday. 5th Sunday in Lent.

The Sunday before Palm Sunday.
Carlins are eaten. These are grey peas, boiled and fried in butter and sugar, and served with rum sauce.

Mr. Moffitt, of Kirkwhelpington, who comes round with flour, brings them uncooked. The inn at Middleton, the only public-house in our district, supplies them cooked.— Various members at Institute Meeting.

Before the war Mr. Moffitt's father used to give a quart of carlins to every customer for Carlin Sunday.—Mrs. Thomas Hepple.

Miss McCracken says that this custom was not known to her when she lived in Scotland, only when she came to Northumberland in 1869. All the public-houses had them.

Owing to an oversight the Editor nearly missed her carlins in 1922, but Mrs. Gilbert Telfer sent her in a dish ready cooked, and very good they were.

The Day Before Good Friday.

When Mrs. Keith was a little girl Mrs. Usher of Cambo House used to give an orange to every child that day, which was the day the school broke up. When her grandfather was at school they used to have a clothes-basket full of ginger snaps given them by somebody. They were made by Peter Brice, the baker, who had his shop near where the Post Office now is, round the corner. Cambo may hardly believe that it ever had a baker, but Mrs. Keith is sure of it because of the story her grandfather told :—Peter Brice kept his donkey in a stable, which had a slit at the donkey's head, and when Peter went in to feed the donkey, the boys of Cambo would frighten the donkey, and then the donkey frightened the old man ! Once somebody came to Mrs. Keith's house on business who said " my great grandfather was baker at Cambo."

Mrs. Keith : " And his name was Peter Brice ! "

Surprised Visitor : " But *you* can't remember him ! "

" Pace or Paste Eggs."

This, like first-footing is almost a universal custom here. " We all dye them."—Miss Emily Charlton, Secretary to the Institute.

This year, 1922, prizes were offered for the three prettiest eggs shown at the W.I. Meeting in April, and twenty-eight sets were exhibited. Onion peeling is largely used, and they are tied up with whin and other flowers, cretonnes, ribbons, wallpapers, etc.

Specimen eggs are kept for years. Mrs. Keith has a dozen eggs on which her grandfather, Mr. Henry Codling, the late joiner, had drawn with a sharp penknife—leaves, swans, a boathouse, a squirrel, owls, and dates from 1882-86. They were dyed with logwood and onion peeling.

In some places in Northumberland the children all come in large numbers on Good Friday and the Saturday to farm-houses and to people who keep hens, and ask for paste eggs. This is not done so much now. The war scarcity checked it. Mrs. Keith always had plenty of eggs but she used to be

B

disappointed that her grandmother would not allow her to go seeking them with the other children.

Mr. George Handyside's sister at Cambo shop used to dye an egg for every child—" rose pink."—Mrs. Hedley.

The children roll their eggs in the field called Chapel Hill, the object is to break other children's and keep your own unbroken.

Mrs. Hedley says they always used to choose a rounded egg, they are less easily broken when " throwing them." " Jauping them " is pushing one against another and if you have an egg with a hard shell you may break two or three.

April Fool's Day.

> " April Fool's Day's past and gone
> You're a Fool and I'm none."

> —Miss Richardson, schoolmistress, Cambo.

" Little things amused us."—Mrs. Hepple.

Miss Shipley says emphatically " It's *minded* " yet.

May Day.

The girls are teased, and asked if they have been up early, and told they won't freckle if they have washed their faces in the dew.—Institute Meeting.

" But I never heard of anybody who did it."—Mrs. Hepple.

Rothley Fair.

" They used to have a *Sunday* fair at Rothley Village, on Whitsunday. They came there on their way from Stagshaw Bank to Rothbury.[1] Just gingerbread, and the usual thing " [but it had clearly been a day of great joy to at least one small boy some seventy years ago].—Mr. George Handyside, shopkeeper, Cambo.

Mrs. Hepple cannot remember the fair itself but remembers that " they used to come through on their way from Stagshaw Bank selling bullets[2] and oranges."

" Mother used to speak of Whitsunday fair when the

[1] Stagshaw Bank was on the Saturday, Rothbury Fair on the Monday.
[2] That is black bullets, peppermints.

mugger tribe set up their stalls at Rothley Town End, yes, near the main road, with gingerbreads, nuts, and all sorts of things."—Mrs. Hedley, whose mother was born at Rothley.

Mr. James Wilkinson says it was " after the tea drinking near the well of Five Lanes End that Morgan used to set up his stall with gingerbreads and sweets at the roadside at Rothley. But the police had him away, at the finish he only stopped without unyoking his horse."

" Five Lanes End " and Stagshaw Bank are a long way from here, but Mr. and Mrs. Wilkinson explain that it was Bor Well Sunday, when they made the tea from a Spa, or spamy well, and there was a great gathering of ladies and gentlemen. They all wore white dresses. It probably goes on still.

Midsummer Day.

The bonfire, or bale, or Baal Fire, at Whalton on Midsummer Day, the longest day of the year, has been kept up from time immemorial,—a year may have been missed during the war. Whalton is about eight miles away.—Miss Brown, farmer, Newbiggin; Mrs. Hepple; Mrs. Hedley.

Barring Out Day.

The following account of the custom is quoted from an old manuscript book written by Mr. Thomas Arkle, of Highlaws, a few miles from here. He died in 1886, aged seventy-nine. He was agent to Lord Decies at Bolam, but came from near Elsdon, an old village on the coaching road between Cambo and Scotland. The book was brought to the Institute Meeting by his granddaughter, Mrs. Handyside, wife of the farmer at Grange Moor, and this passage was read aloud.

" In country places it was formerly the custom for the Scholars to assemble in the Schoolroom early in the morning of St. Thomas's Day, when the door was barricaded in order to secure the exclusion of the Master till the periods were settled over which the Christmas and Easter Holidays were to extend. Upon this, the ' Barring Out Day ' all authority was subverted, the school became a scene of tumultuous merriment, the Dominie on his arrival was assailed with jests, and freedoms were taken which at any other time the most forward boys would never have attempted. A paper containing the terms on which admittance could be obtained was thrust out below the door, generally providing for so many days play at Christmas and Easter and in many cases containing a provision that the Scholars were to be allowed the privilege of attending all the Horse racings and Cockfights in the locality, gatherings which were then neither few nor far between. The door was resolutely kept fast till the Constitutions were either accepted as first proposed, or a modified treaty concluded to the satisfaction of both parties.

The following is a copy of the terms proposed by Scholars at Elsdon in 1826, the only year as far as I remember in which rhyme was attempted.

> Here's dark December's raging blast;
>   The year's now flown on rapid wings.
> We've closed the door we'll keep it fast
>   Until we know what Christmas brings.
>
> This custom's liv'd from age to age
>   And will exist in time to come.
> So you must cease to stamp and rage;
>   And strive to keep your passion down.
>
> You often beat us with a strap
>   Which makes us feel the keenest pain
> And then pin ' Dunce ' upon our back
>   To work us further grief and shame.
>
> This day hath heightened all our joys
>   To think we have you at command.
> How pleased the little girls and boys
>   To see you outside shiv'ring stand.
>
> We have agreed to nine days' play
>   And Cockfights, Races to attend
> Likewise a week at Easter day
>   Pray, Sir, accept the terms we send."

At the Institute Meeting the schoolmistress at Cambo told us it had been done *once* in her time, and once in her predecessor's, Mr. Irving's; and when one of the Vice-Presidents asked if any guilty children were present the hands of several members went up, including that of our Institute Secretary, Miss Charlton, who gives the following account:

" We did it after dinner on the shortest day, and Mr.

Irving came and locked the girls' door outside, we'd bolted it inside. The boys had locked their door outside so he couldn't lock that, so he tied it to the scraper, but one of the boys squeezed out of the little window by the porch and let us out."

Her father reports that " we did it *every* year to Mr. Brown in the old school in the village hall on the shortest day of the year after dinner; he would go round and tap at the windows, and then he would go home, and we would go home too."

Mrs. Hedley says of one such occasion:

" There were a lot of big boys then, they went to school in winter, and worked out all the summer; they brought a lot of ropes to school that day, and there were a lot of forms, and they tied all three doors, and put forms in front. Mr. Brown got one door a little open, and broke a blade of his favourite penknife trying to cut the rope, and that made him very angry, and when he got in he did thrash them. I *was* frightened. I would be in the Infants, or Standard I."

It will be seen that the custom was deeply rooted, and would probably have been in existence still if it had not " been stopped."

> " *The 29th of May,*
> *Royal Oak Day,*
> If you don't give us holiday
> We'll all run away."

Miss Bella Wilson[1] as a child was one of the schoolful who last tried to " run away "; it was on the 29th of May, and never again. On that day Charles II hid in the oak amongst leaves.

Christmas Time.

Carol singers used to go round.

Houses are *decorated with holly, mistletoe, ivy, and yew.*—Members at Institute Meeting.

Mrs. Keith has described to us the following features of Christmas when she was a child:—

Fromerty made with barley, etc.

Yule dollies made of pastry, a man with his arms crossed, with currants for buttons.

[1] Now Mrs. E. Hedley.

She remembers the old saying:—

> " Dames get up and bake your pies
> And let your lazy maidens lie
> On Christmas Day in the morning."

Bread and cheese were given to visitors on Christmas Day, and New Year's Day.

The *Yule log* on Christmas Eve was lit with the ashes of the log of the previous Christmas.

Mrs. Robert Hepple, wife of the farmer, tells us that the Yule log is always lit with the ashes of the old one at Rugley Walls still.

Her mother-in-law, Mrs. Thomas Hepple, says that in her old home at Cambo, before her marriage, they always had a Yule log, but it was her husband who was particular that the Yule log should be taken off before it was burnt out, and should be put on again the following Christmas Eve, and burnt out then before the new one was put on. " My mother always made Yule Dollies, I don't make them now." " Fromerty is boiled barley, milk and sugar. There was an old joiner at Wallington called Charlton, who always had fromerty every Christmas Eve."

Mrs. Robert Hepple says that everybody at her old home used to *stir the plum pudding and wish a wish*, but they don't at Rugley Walls. There is a pinch of salt in the plum pudding, but she doesn't know why. Mrs. Robert Hepple's family, the Murrays of Rothley Park Farm, have been there and at other farms in the district, Gallowshill and Elf Hills, for generations. She had a Scotch great-grandmother, and Murray is a Scotch name, but she doesn't know how far back.

Miss Gow says that in her home the plum pudding is stirred by everybody in the house. She thinks that a pinch of salt is, or used to be, put into the plum pudding, and that the origin of this was to avert the evil eye.

Miss Gow's father was Scotch, and her mother from the Otterburn neighbourhood.

" We all stir the plum pudding," the Hedleys of the Post Office say.

" When you have the first mince pie you must wish a wish."—Miss Hilda Hedley.

Guisers.

" They haven't gone guising here for a long time," " They

used to come from Kirkwhelpington," so they say in Cambo.
" We used to go guising when we were lads with masks
on our faces and tall hats, and went from house to house
singing," said Mr. James Batey of Kirkwhelpington, a mason,
who is often working in Cambo.   All he could remember
of the Guisers' little play is—

> " Here comes Dr. Brown
> The best doctor in the town."

Mr. James Thornton of Scots Gap says much the same as
Mr. Batey about his boyhood, in our district.

" I've seen the first-footers here come guised with masks
on."—Mrs. Hepple.

" They used to do it at Woodburn and Otterburn." [1]

The Sword Dancers.

According to Mrs. Keith, Guisers and Sword Dancers are
closely akin.   " Almost the first thing I can remember was
when we lived at the Dovecot, and Sword Dancers came at
the New Year, in the dark, and danced the sword dance in
the back yard by the light of lanterns, all dressed up,—there
was old Betty, and Nelson, and a doctor; and after they'd
finished the dance one held up all the swords.   They came
from about Boghall.[2]   Yes, miners and the lads about.   They
used to come from Blaydon too.[3]   They were given ginger
wine, and cake." [4]

[1] In our childhood, in the eighties, at the little village of Rock, near
Alnwick, thirty miles to the north-east, Guisers came every year in
December before Christmas, and did a fragment of an old play,—S.
George and other characters were introduced, there was a pretence of
fighting, and the doctor was important.   They were all lads from the
village or farms, but we never could tell which they were.—Miss R. E.
Bosanquet and Miss J. D. Carr, Cambo.

[2] Three miles away.

[3] Farther off.

[4] As children we used to see the Sword Dancers at Christmas parties
at Alnwick Castle and elsewhere.   They came from Earsdon and other
places, and their song is given by John Stokoe.   " Songs and Ballads
of Northern England," p. 154.
    Within the last few days we have seen the Winlaton Sword
Dancers at Bellingham Agricultural Show, eighteen miles away.   They
were the winning team out of eleven at the Newcastle Musical Festival
this year, 1922.   Betty, five Sword Dancers, an introducer, and a pipe
player formed the company of eight.—Miss J. D. Carr and Miss R. E.
Bosanquet.

Hogmanay or Agmanay.

" When we came guising father and mother used to say :—

To-night, to-night is old year's night,
To-morrow is New Year's Day.
Get up, old wives, and shake your feathers.
And don't you think that we are old beggars.
We are only girls and boys come out to play,
Please give us a piece and we'll away.
We haven't come to your house to beg or to borrow,
But we've come to your house to wash away all sorrow,
With our pockets full of money and ourselves full of cheer
I wish you've had a merry Christmas and a prosperous New
    Year."

—Miss Graham, helped by Mrs. Graham, Wallington.

The parents came here from Cumberland twenty years ago,
and the word there seems to be " Agmanay."

Mrs. Hepple and Miss Shipley do not know this rhyme, the
only one they have heard is :—" Here's my sonce, and here's
my sele, and here's my *Hogmanay*," which was sometimes
said at the New Year.

Mrs. Hedley says that Hogmanay is a Scotch custom, but
the Editor remembers it when she was a child at Rock.

CHAPTER II

BUILDING AND FARMING CUSTOMS

" COUPLE Beer " was the name given to the beer or spirits, which it was customary to give to the masons and joiners when the first couple was hoisted. All that sort of thing has gradually come to an end.—Mr. James Batey, mason. (Works often at Cambo. Lives at Kirkwhelpington.)

The omission of this custom caused one house to be called " Drythropple "; it is a house about six miles from Alnwick. Miss Richardson and Miss R. E. Bosanquet have always heard this explanation of the name in that neighbourhood; the latter heard it from her father, Charles B. P. Bosanquet of Rock, who died in 1905, aged seventy.

Haymaking and Stents.

Cambo West Field is divided by a row of hollies, " the cows belonging to the people in the village were in the field to the north of the hollies, the hayfields were to the south. Everybody kept a cow then. Every family had their hay sticked out, and they had the same bit every year, and had to win it themselves. Yes, it was a very old custom, and went on till Mr. Gow came [in 1847]. After that they had to pay £10 a year for a cow, that is £5 rent, and £5 for the hay, but the hay was won for them. They have the old custom still at Netherwitton." [1]

The West Field is still sometimes called " The Cottagers' Field." [2]—Mr. George Charlton, woodman, Close House.

Mrs. Handyside, wife of the farmer at Grange Moor, says that she lived at Netherwitton as a child. " They call them

---

[1] Five or six miles from Cambo.
[2] See also Chapter XXVI, p. 175.

stents there," which she supposes is the same word as "Stints." "They were divided by sticks, and sometimes for fun we children would pull up the sticks and hide them."

"Sir Walter [Trevelyan] had a lot of prize cattle, and he had one hundred and forty or one hundred and fifty acres under hay. I've seen ten or eleven pikes going up, and three workers at each in the pit field. Everybody in Cambo used to work out [during haymaking], all the wives too. Some of the men only had 15s. a week, there was more barter then. In the beginning of Sir Walter's time, it was all done with the hand rake."—Mr. George Charlton.

When most of us were children the kiles of hay used to be drawn together by two horses with a rope between them, and the heaviest man, and all the children riding on the hay; there was a delicious fear that the next moment might land us all in a heap amongst the great horse hoofs, but it never did, the heaviest man was always able to keep us safe. In the last few years a hay trailer has been introduced which trails the kiles together without the children, then it is still made into pikes, one worker standing on the top and others forking the hay. Each pike is made firm with hay ropes and left standing till the sap has gone out of the hay and it is sufficiently dry for stacking. Then each pike is drawn on to a low bogey, and taken home to the stackyard with a party of children squeezed on behind.—Miss R. E. Bosanquet and Mrs. Handyside.

Harvest Customs.

The farms round Cambo are almost entirely grass farms now, so the harvest customs refer to the old days when "there was tillage." [1]

"I can remember when corn was grown here,—corn and turnips by the Saugh House."—Mr. George Charlton.

"Sir Walter had valuable cattle, and grew corn, wheat, and barley and oats, and turnips."—Mrs. Pearson, the Dovecot, aged seventy-seven.

"At harvest time the farmers used all to drive in to Cambo

[1] In this connection Mr. George Thornton's poem on Greenleighton on p. 49 should be read; it shows how in 1842 hay time and harvest were of importance on the very edge of the fells.

in carts to get workers, and the labourers' wives, my mother amongst them, would jump out of one cart into another to go with the farmer who offered them the most money. My father's money was only 14s. a week. It was only 12s. before Mr. Gow came. Of course they had a cow, and there were *cow clubs* which were a great help if the cow died. They used to shear the corn with a sickle, both women and men. And they said *the one that got the last sheaf would be the first married*; I don't know if they were! Yes, the one that cut the last sheaf. The men used to have a month's harvest. And I've seen them make a *kern babby* out of a sheaf with a skirt on it, and carry it round the field. There was dancing at the *kern suppers*, in the barn by the blacksmith's shop at Cambo, between his house and shop; it's a byre now, I think."—Mrs. Thomas Hepple.

They still parade the village at Whalton[1] with the kern babby, it was said at an Institute Meeting.

Mrs. Charles Trevelyan,[2] President of the Institute, says that she has seen the kern dolly hanging up in a sitting-room at the Robsons' farm at Sweethope.[3]

Miss McCracken remembers the following harvest custom in Ayrshire before she came to live in Northumberland in 1869 —the girls, blindfolded, tried to cut the last piece of corn with the sickle,—just a handful—not a sheaf; the one who cut it hung it up above the door, and the name—that is the Christian name—of the first man who came in was supposed to be the name of the man she should marry. She remembers a man who was a stranger coming to their door, and a maid coming to her mother and asking her to ask him his name, and first he gave his surname, and her mother said no, it was the Christian name she wanted.

Miss Richardson remembers the men coming to ask her mother to lead in the last load of corn on their farm, the Lee Moor, near Alnwick.

Ploughing with Oxen.

The great park at Wallington has not been ploughed since it was ploughed by oxen, as can be seen by the wide curve at the end of the rig.—Mr. Edward Keith, head gardener, Wallington.

[1] Whalton is a few miles away.
[2] Now Lady Trevelyan.
[3] A few miles away.

" *They used to flail the corn* at Broom House, I can mind that, and they had a cheese vat. They used to make butter and cheese."—Mr. George Handyside, whose uncle, Mr. Richardson, farmed Broom House, many years back.

Miss Mitchell, Mr. George Handyside's housekeeper, says that when she was a child on a farm in Aberdeenshire they used to flail the corn in winter when the water wheel, which drove the thrashing machine, was frozen. Two men would work together keeping time with their strokes. She used to *try* to do it.

" My grandfather used to say that he engaged a man in the winter to do the flailing, and they had a board and laid it on to."—Miss Shanks, Cambo.

Mrs. Rutherford understood that they used to set the doors open when they were flailing.

The following Wages List was found fastened inside the little door of a bureau, in the hand-writing of Mr. John Tate, who bought Barnhill, Guyzance, in 1862. Our member Mrs. Carr-Ellison is a niece of his.

Barnhill Wages.

Thos. Allison . 13/6 a week.
30 Stones of Flour.
30 Stones of Oatmeal.
50 Stones of Mixt. Meal.
Full lot of Potatoes.

James Chambers 15/- a week.
Half lot of Potatoes.

Robt. Hall . . 15/- a week.
Half lot of Potatoes.

John Hall . . 14/- a week.
Half lot of Potatoes.

James Howey . 14/6 a week.
Half lot of Potatoes.

William Tate . 8/- a week.
                9 Bushels of Wheat.
                12 Bushels of Barley.
                6 Bushels of Pease.
                25 Bushels of Oatmeal.
                Cow kept.
                Half lot of Potatoes.

Shilbottle.

J. Richardson . 15/- a week, Cow and Potatoes.
R. Kirkup . . 15/- a week and Half lot of Potatoes.
F. Green . . 12/- a week, Cow, and Half lot of Potatoes.
Joe Richardson 12/- a week for summer half year.

(" Barnhill bought in 1862 shortly before J. T. married, according to Mary Apperley's Book (?)."—Note by Mr. T. Tate of Bank House, Acklington, where the bureau now is.)

The *Hirings, payment of wages in kind,* and *Ploughing Day* were discussed at an Institute Meeting when farmers, and members of farming and shepherds' families were present; the following amongst others took part in the discussion or gave information at other times on this subject.

Miss Brown, farmer, Newbiggin.
Mrs. Handyside, wife of farmer, Grange Moor.
Mr. Walter Hedley, shepherd, Cambo, and his daughter.
Mr. John Henderson, farmer, Scots Gap.
Mr. Robert Hepple, farmer, Rugley Walls.
Mr. F. W. Greswell, estate agent, Cambo.
Miss Murray, daughter of farmer, Rothley Park.
Mrs. Truelove, Cambo, sister of farmer and shepherds.
Miss McCracken, Saugh House, Vice-President of W.I.

The March Hiring in Morpeth on the first Wednesday in March is for farm workers, married men who are *hinds* and their families.

The *shepherds* are engaged earlier, soon after the New Year.

Both hinds and shepherds are engaged for a year from the May Term, the 12th of May to the 12th of May, *Flitting Day,* when they move if they are going to work for another farmer. The farmer to whom they are going sends carts for them and their furniture. If a farmer wishes to re-engage his men he speaks to them the night before Morpeth Hiring, if he wishes to make a change he says nothing. If they cannot come to terms about a change of wages over night they often do so at the Hirings. Many people go in to the Hirings, merely to see their friends. It is a holiday.

The May Hiring is on the first Wednesday in May, in Morpeth. It is for the unmarried lads and girls who live in the farmhouses. They are engaged for six months; there are hirings again in November. The actual change is made on May 12th or 13th and on November 11th. These May hirings are also very festive occasions,—" stalls in the streets, merry-go-rounds, Aunt Sally, Cocoanut shies, such a crowd you could hardly move."—Miss Alice Coombes, parlourmaid.[1]

Those wishing to be hired stand in the market place, and in the hall below, and it is difficult for a stranger to distinguish the wouldbe maids from the onlookers. " We spoke to anybody we thought looked likely."—Mrs. Grant and Miss McCracken.

The lads who wanted work on tillage land used to wear an ear of corn in their hat, and those who wanted work as shepherds a piece of wool.—Mr. J. Hedley.

At all the Hirings the agreement is as a rule only by word of mouth, but the bargain is closed by the farmer or his wife giving " arles ";[2] if they break the bargain they are supposed to send back the arles, but a story is told of a girl who went round giving different names and engaging herself to several people, and made quite a lot! Half a crown is often the amount given as arles. " I'd never like to offer as little as 1s."

Miss McCracken remembers her father coming back from Bellingham Hirings years ago, and saying that a girl had refused a half-crown saying it was unlucky, and had taken 2s. Nobody else had heard of 2s. 6d. being unlucky.

Payment of Wages in kind.

On the hills even now shepherds are sometimes paid entirely in stock, and throughout this district shepherds are sometimes paid partly in stock and partly in money; they have the privilege of running so many sheep and lambs of their

---

[1] Now Mrs. J. Tait.
[2] Money given in confirmation of a bargain.

own with the masters. The saying is " a shepherd's pack never dies! " and " whilst he is looking after his own pack he looks after the farmer's! " The auctioneers sell the shepherd's pack free of commission.

The settlement of wages is often only half yearly or yearly. One speaker said of unmarried hinds—of whom there are many here living in the farmhouses—" if you get a good man he'll never ask for any wages till the end of the agreement." Once a month or once a fortnight is very usual in the case of married hinds.

In the present day the married hind gets his house rent free, and his coals, as a part of his wages. When there was a lot of ploughed land here the hinds had their 1,000 yards of potatoes, which they or their families took up themselves, —as is still the case in the rest of Northumberland.

In the past the hinds were sometimes paid entirely in kind; sometimes partly in kind, and only a little money. The keep of a cow used to be included, also a sack of oatmeal; so much barley is still included in some places. This point is illustrated by the wages list given on page 28.

Mr. Walter Hedley explains that a shepherd has to buy his own sheep, but he gets his wages when he " casts them "— in their price—and in their wool. They run them " through and through," that is the shepherd like the farmer has sheep of every age, and they run together so he is always amongst them all. The saying is " the shepherd's sheep are always the best! " And Mrs. Hedley adds " the farmers are very good, they always give a good price for the shepherd's sheep, they give them a good start." In some places, however, they are sold with the master's at the same price.

" The lambing cow " is the cow which the farmer supplies to the shepherd at lambing time so that he need not use the milk of his own cow for the lambs.—Mr. Walter Hedley.

Ploughing Day still goes on.

[At Scarlett Hall, when Mr. Arthur Dixon came in, the farmers round sent horses and ploughs for a day to give him a start.]

Fields.

The fields were much smaller then [the first half of the

nineteenth century] than they are now, three fields then where there is one now. They were known by the names of those who had them,—Hepple's field, Dodd's field, etc.—Mr. George Charlton.

Horse Brasses.

Some of the hinds have handsome brass ornaments for their horses' harness; one such set for a pair of horses was shown us by Mrs. Finlay, wife of a hind, at Grange Moor Farm. Crescents and stars, and hearts, are favourite patterns in the metal work. There are also brass bells, rosettes, and ribbons of many colours for agricultural and other shows, and special occasions.

CHAPTER III

" *Baby Customs and Superstitions.*

In the olden days before District Nurses were in vogue young mothers had to depend on the help of their kind neighbours. Those elderly people as a rule were very superstitious and the first thing debated after Baby's birth was usually *the luck of the natal day.* Certain days were looked upon as decidedly lucky, others doubtful. The following rhyme is well known in Northumberland :—

> Born on Monday, fair of face,
> Born on Tuesday, full of God's grace,
> Born on Wednesday, merry and glad,
> Born on Thursday, sour and sad,
> Born on Friday, godly given,
> Born on Saturday, work for your living,
> Born on Sunday, never shall want,
> There's the week and the end on't.

In *dressing the child* (up to its Baptism) the clothes must be drawn on from the feet upwards, also the nails must not be cut.

The Christening Day.

On the way to the Church a parcel of food is given to the first person met and they are expected to give in return a small silver coin for luck.

On being *taken into a neighbour's house for the first time,* the baby is usually given three things, a pinch of salt, a piece of bread and a silver coin and sometimes a match."—Written down by Mrs. Keith.

" I've heard them say *you shouldn't cut a baby's nails* till

33   c

it can bite them itself."—Mrs. Thomas Hepple and Miss Shipley.

" I've heard Mother say that and all, and more than Mother say it. I've heard often that."—Mrs. Thomas Hepple.

Mrs. Hedley has heard that " you shouldn't cut a baby's nails,—not till it is christened," she thinks.

" They say you *mustn't take a baby into another house till it has been christened*."—Miss Catherine Hedley.

Mrs. Hepple says the parcel of spice loaf and cheese was given to the first person met on the way to Church. " When my son was christened we met Jack Green, the blacksmith, who was courting Mrs. Gow's cook, and *made* them take it. They say *it's unlucky if they don't take it*."

" It is *carried by the same person who carries the baby*. It was called the *cheese and bread*, and there was always cheese, but some of the cakes *for the tea* would be put in instead of the bread."—Mrs. Hedley.

She thinks the custom is dropping out now, but had evidently done it for her children.

" A piece of cake and a piece of cheese."—Mrs. Robert Wilson, wife of butcher.

" It is *lucky to be given it*, they are supposed to get some of *the baby's beauty!* "—Mrs. Truelove, widow of butler.

Christening Cakes and Teas are usual to-day. When one of our members gave a demonstration recently in cake icing, the iced cake was bought for a christening cake by a young mother, who is also a member.

The *first time a baby comes to see you*, you must give it *three things*,—salt, egg, and a biscuit or a bit of bread. " That was Mother's way."—Mrs. Thomas Hepple.

She seems to lay stress on the number three rather than on the exact things.

Mrs. Edward Pearson, the Dovecot, widow of joiner, thinks that an egg, a teacake, and a bit of salt are right, but also lays stress on *three* things rather than on the exact things— just lately she gave a little handkerchief instead of the salt to a baby.

" The first time a baby comes to visit you it must be given salt, egg, 6d. or some bit of money, and sometimes a bit of bread."—Mrs. Hedley.

" An egg, salt and 6d. in a bag is what I always give, my mother's mother told me."—Mrs. Robert Wilson.

Mrs. Edwin Pearson, Cambo, who came from Redcar, and married into an old Cambo family, says, " When Edwina was going to be christened thirteen years ago, I couldn't understand what they meant when they asked if I'd made up the parcel for the lucky one, but they explained to me, and I've always done it since. If we don't meet anybody on the way we give it to the clergyman, or to the one that pours the water into the font. Yes, my babies are given the presents the first time they go to another house. But I'm not superstitious, I always let my children go anywhere, even before they're christened, and they've always been lucky."

> " Thumb ikkle,
> Lick Pot,
> Long Man,
> Strong man,
> Little Tom Tidy man."

Rhymes told to a baby on its fingers. Mrs. Pearson of the Dovecot used to say it to Mrs. Keith when Mrs. Keith was a child.

WEDDING CUSTOMS

In the year 1839 my mother (Elizabeth Hedley) was married. The *marriage* was solemnized in Bellingham[1] Presbyterian Church. Following the fashion of those days, the Bride and Bridegroom rode away from the church on horseback. The *guests raced* to Tarset Hall,[1] the home of the bride, and the first gentleman to arrive had the honour of *kissing the Bride,* who in return pinned a rosette to his coat. Two violinists played as the guests entered the house.—Mrs. Joseph Hall, Scots Gap, widow of coachman, written down by her daughter Miss Jessie Hall.[2]

" Before Cambo Church was built[3] when the weddings were at Hartburn, they used to *ride the kail* to Cambo. George Charlton was telling me."—Mrs. Ephraim Hedley, wife of farmer, Elf Hills.

" Anthony Dunn of Raff Shiel rode for the kail from

[1] Bellingham and Tarset are on the North Tyne many miles from Cambo.
[2] Now Mrs. Walter Young.
[3] Cambo Church was consecrated in 1843.

Hartburn to Gallowshill.   Yes, he won *the prize*—the *bride's garter*,[1] or something like it, say a ribbon.   The first home got the garter.   It was our grandmother's and grandfather's wedding.   She was from Wingates, but the wedding was from Gallowshill.   She jumped over the petting stool at Hartburn. It was the year Queen Victoria was married."—Miss Murray.

" Polly and Nelly Brown's father rode the kail at Bolam, and got hurt against an iron gate.   I was a child, and wasn't there, but I remember coming in, and hearing them say that Nicholas had got hurt riding the kail, that would be about fifty years ago.   It was at the wedding of his brother Lancelot who was marrying a Miss Hall near Gallowhill.[2]   He died two or three years ago."—Mrs. Armstrong, wife of joiner, Cambo.

Miss Mary Brown, the Portico, Wallington, has asked her aunt at the Raw, a farm near Elsdon, about this, and is told that " *the kail was a bottle of whisky*—you galloped from the Church, got a bottle of whisky at the house, and a glass, and galloped back to meet the bride and bridegroom, and then got a present from the bride,—her glove, or a brooch or some small thing.   They rode a great deal in those days, because of the rough roads.   My aunt used to ride to Church on horseback with white stockings and black shoes."

Miss Brown's father farmed Foulmart Law, Bolam; he came there from the Raw, Elsdon, where his family have been for five hundred years.   The farmhouse at the Raw is not an old one.   They were at Laings Hill, a neighbouring farm, part of the time.   In the Elsdon Registers, which begin in 1672, Nicholas Brown was buried in 1675, and the names Lancelot and Nicholas Brown figure at intervals afterwards.   They are the same family as Sir Lancelot Brown, *Capability Brown*, a man famous in Cambo history, who went to school here and laid out Capheaton, Kirk Harle, lakes at Dalton and gardens in other places.   Elsdon is outside our district, but the family is thus closely connected with Cambo both in the eighteenth century and to-day.

Compare both Hodgson and Mackenzie for other details of

---

[1] Compare Thomas Whittell's poem, " The Rape of the Garter," the marriage of Ben Rickey of Rothley at Hartburn Church, written in the early eighteenth century.   The marriage was on May 21st, 1721.

[2] Bolam, not the Gallowshill of the previous story.   Bolam is outside our district.

Capability Brown. Mr. Perceval of Long Witton had the Brown pedigree. See Appendix A.

Mrs. Thomas Hepple discussed " riding for the kail." She knew Anthony Dunn, but did not remember the story of that particular occasion. " They would have *some broth* when they got there," said Mrs. Hepple; " *a few kail* as they called it," added Miss Shipley.

Miss Shipley is ninety-three and Mrs. Hepple eighty: Mrs. Hepple was christened at Hartburn Church, her next brother at Cambo. That and the statement of the late Rev. C. A. Fitch fixes the date of the building and consecration of Cambo Church as 1842 and 1843.

" The groom and clerk had white ribbons."—Mrs. Hepple.

" At Cambo they always make the Churchyard gate fast, they tie it up so that they have to pay to come through; the children do it, and then they have to throw pennies for them. When Johnson Nixon was here he used to wire it! "—Mrs. Keith.

" They generally have two groomsmen and two bridesmaids. They throw rice and an old shoe, and I remember at Kirkwhelpington a shoe being tied to the carriage. In many places they have the petting stool to jump over but not at Cambo." —Miss Lucy Foster,[1] daughter of farmer, Whitehill.

The Institute Meeting agreed that one ought to put a bit of *wedding cake under one's pillow* and sleep on it.

In some places a bit of *china* is *thrown* over the bride's head as she goes into the house, and it is unlucky if it does not break; one version is that she must throw up her hand and break the china; a plate was thrown at a recent wedding in the district, but it is not a Cambo custom, though it is in other parts of Northumberland.

At a wedding you're supposed *to wear:*—

> " Something borrowed
> Something blue
> Something old
> And something new."
> —Mrs. Keith.[2]

Mrs. Keith came and borrowed a prayer book for her own

---

[1] Now Mrs. Robert Stephenson.
[2] See also Chapter VI, p. 83, for custom of planting rosemary.

wedding,—one of Mrs. Hedley's family had a new one to lend her.

" If a younger sister gets married before the elder one, they say the older one must *dance* at the wedding *in* her *stocking feet*."—Miss Hilda Hedley, confirmed by Mrs. Hedley.

A member of the Institute—Miss J. D. Carr—has large pieces of the *wedding dress*, worn by her great-great-grandmother, Miss Isabella Byne, at her wedding to Ralph Carr at Ponteland[1] in 1758; it is a rich brocade, cream ground with large flowers in red and green.

FUNERAL CUSTOMS

" The long *crape hatbands* that were worn were very wide, a foot or eighteen inches, with a big bow at the back of the hats, tied with ribbon (they didn't put the crape through), black for a man, white for a woman or girl; white gloves for young people. The long crape hatbands were a great expense, and it is a very good thing it has gone out. I've never tied one, but Mother must have tied scores. It was when I was quite a little girl.

The serving of *cake and wine*, and also the handing out of memory cards, before the funeral, is going out."—Mrs. Hedley.

A few years ago a young girl died at Newbiggin and she asked that Miss Emily Charlton, and others of her girl friends should be the bearers, and they wore *white scarves*.

" They don't seem to make as much of funerals now."—Miss Bella Wilson.

" When we first came to live in Northumberland in 1869 at Blackhall,[2] I remember a *bidder* coming to invite my father to a funeral. I think it was the funeral of old Mr. —— of Whitehill. He had long hat bands."—Miss McCracken.

" They used to come at Cambo, too, wearing long crape hat bands. They used to give *gloves* and long hat bands. I'm not sure if it was to the bearers. My father used to get them."—Mrs. Forster, Whitehill.

" They used to have long crape bands for the men's hats,

---

[1] Ponteland is about fourteen miles away. Miss Isabella Byne was great-great-grandmother to Miss R. E. Bosanquet also.
[2] Some miles away.

hanging down behind, and these and a pair of gloves were given to every mourner. I remember when I was a child my father went to the funeral of old Miss Harle at Low Angerton,[1] where Mrs. Leathart lives now, and besides the crape bands, and gloves, they were each given a black scarf to put over one shoulder and under the other arm, and it was such beautiful silk. Funerals were a great expense. The scarves were tied with white for young people, and with black for old people. The streamers gradually got shorter."—Miss Brown.

" At Morpeth[2] the bell tolls when anybody has died. I think it is nine for a man. It's the bell in the clock tower in the middle of the town."—Miss Murray.

[1] A few miles away.
[2] Our Market Town, twelve miles away.

CHAPTER IV

CHANGES IN SOCIAL AND ECONOMIC LIFE AND CUSTOM

THE WEAVERS

MR. JOHN WILKINSON, now living at Longwitton, who is in his eightieth year, says that Hartington Hall " was let out in tenements and a lot of people lived there, principally weavers. It was a tremendous long time ago; it would be before the Forsters' time,[1] about the troublesome times. The real farmhouse used to be where the stables are, but it was the Hall which was let out in tenements."

Repeated by his brother, Mr. James Wilkinson, who is in his seventy-seventh year, and was born at Hartington, and " wrought for " [2] the Forsters.

There is a stone at the edge of the river Hart,—very smooth and flat on the top, which is still called " the Knocking Stone "; " that is where they used to beat the web."—Mr. James Wilkinson.

The stone is opposite his cottage, and only a stone's throw from the Hall. The only weaver he remembers is old Andra Pearson, but there was another at Middleton, he says, named Waitt.

Old Andra Pearson,[3] who fought in the Peninsular War, and is grandfather, or great-grandfather to many people in and around Cambo, was apprenticed to a weaver, and at the end of his soldiering, about 1815, he took up weaving again to eke out other earnings. His granddaughter, Mrs.

---

[1] Mrs. Trevelyan tells us that the Forsters had been at Hartington Hall for two hundred years; the last farmer of that name, Mr. George Forster, died in 1907, aged eighty-eight, a fine old man.

[2] " Worked for."

[3] Further particulars of him are given under the heading of Stories, Chapter XVI, pp. 116, 117.

Hedley at Cambo Post Office, has a hand towel beautifully woven by him, and marked in small letters " A.M.P." for Andrew and Mary Pearson. " He wove the Grange Moor linen."—Mrs. Hedley.

Miss Shanks' grandfather used to speak of weavers at Bavington.

CAMBO IN 1842

To-day in Cambo (1922) we are fortunate in having a blacksmith's shop, a butcher's shop, a joiner, one grocer's and draper's shop with a tailor at work above, and a Post Office; there is a shoemaker half a mile away at Close House; the Temperance Hotel is at Scots Gap, near the Railway Station, a mile away. But the following poem shows how many more tradesmen there were in 1842.

LINES ON CAMBO, 1842 AND 1894

Sweet Cambo, village standing high
　　And proudly looking down
Towards the Wansbeck's crystal floods
　　That flows from Wannies' hills so brown,
And overlooks the wooded plains
　　Of pleasant Wallington's domains.

When first I saw this village fair
　　How different then from now,
Its populace of tradesmen full—
　　To changing time its had to bow,
In eighteen forty-two or three
　　I first this lovely place did see.

The Blacksmith, with his " brawny " arm
　　Did thunder at the forge,
To keep the teams of farmers trim
　　It was to him a daily charge,
For every farm had tillage then,
　　And all did need some ploughing men.

The Saddler, here found work to do
　　To make the needed " gears "
That cultivation of the land
　　Demanded new, likewise repairs,
In the back row his shop was seen
　　The roof of thatch, in front a green.

The Butcher here the ox did slay
   The ovine " wedder " prime
And fourpence halfpenny per pound
   The current price was at that time,
No infant mutton, did he kill
   This was beneath Sir Cleaver's skill.

The Clogger, he did labour here
   And busy was he too
The useful feet on maids and men
   To cover with the wooden shoe
To follow up their daily toil
   As honest tillers of the soil.

The Cooper, here, he found employ
   Did butter firkins make
But now, the cows, like working men
   Are scarce provided with a " stake "
On all the vast outstretch of land
   Where scarce is seen a working hand.

No: Denmark sends us butter now
   Why should we troubled be?
The Swiss, they send us tons of milk.
   Thus farmers now, they quite agree
To pay the landlords' plenty rent—
   For men and cows,—tis banishment.

A Doctor, here, did labour too,
   Drew blood and gave a pill,
He always did the lancet use
   On those that felt a little ill,
Such practice now, would not be borne
   Æsculapius modern, would scorn,

The very thought of draining out
   The crimson fluid of life,
Still then, as now, the people lived
   Yea, battled on amidst the strife
For years beyond the Scripture span
   That is allotted out to man.

The Grocer too, was busy kept
   His patrons to supply,
His sugar, coffee, rice and tea
   Were good, none better you could buy
And still his name is on the sign
   And may it still remain some time.

And then, this village had an Inn
  The sign board lofty swung,
Whereon the " Queens " were painted gay,
  Queen Mary, her whom sorrow wrung
Fair Scotia's unfortunate Queen,
  On the North side of board was seen.

And on the sunny Southern side
  Elizabeth appeared
The " good Queen Bess " of centuries gone
  Whom her dear subjects much revered,
Displayed were these, that at the shrine
  Hearts might bow, to the god of wine.

The Joiner had his part to do
  And well employed was he,
The farmers then, with tillage land
  Caused him, with them, to often be,
Their rollers, carts and harrows, were
  Often needing a bit repair.

And here was one to make the shoes
  A first rate maker too,
I've seen him have six men employed
  Beside himself, so much to do.
A blythe and sturdy man was he,
  In business prompt, as men should be.

And here, the Tailor clothes provide
  For little boys and men
From Melton cloth, and Scottish tweeds
  You need but mention how and when
And he will you a suit provide
  Surpassed by none, in country wide.

And here did dwell the Teacher sage
  In form both tall and straight.
Who towered high 'mongst teachers then
  In lore he was a man of weight,
And well did he the same impart
  To many a youthful loving heart.

Lines written in 1894 by the late George Thornton, Star View,
Rothbury (formerly of Ewesley Station).

Copied from his own manuscript, belonging to his sister-
in-law, Mrs. Pearson of the Dovecot, to whom he had sent
it. He was born in 1835, died about 1918.

He was the first man about here to make a bicycle and a tricycle. He made one with carriage attached, and used to take his wife to Church at Rothbury till they had an accident. —Mr. George Shade, gamekeeper, Wallington.

There are many reasons why the Cambo of 1842 had more " tradesmen " than the same village in 1922.

One reason—the change of surrounding country from tillage to grassland—has been mentioned in connection with farming customs.

Another reason—the changes from riding and coaching to bicycling, railway travelling and motoring will be referred to later.

But first we give a few details of various industries and occupations which there have been in and around Cambo.

The Saddler.

Miss Murray has a copy of the *Newcastle Courant*, 1867, in which the sale is advertised of Mr. John Gibson, saddler and ironmonger, Cambo, who is retiring from business. He was the last saddler at Cambo.

The Shoemakers.

" When we were at school at Cambo we could see the shoemakers upstairs where the Post Office now stands. The ground floor was a hemmel." [1]—Mrs. Pearson.

Coopers.

We have been told that there used to be a cooper at Cambo, and a cooper at Rothley,—only about two miles apart, and coopers at Bavington, and we therefore asked why there were so many coopers.

" There were so many wooden things; there were the skeels in which the women carried the water on their heads, —they had a handle on one side; the bowls for the milk were all wooden, and the butter firkins, so were the pails for water, and to feed the calves; I've given the poss-tub[2] to my grandfather to take to the cooper to be new bottomed.

Everybody had a cow, and a great deal of butter was made. My grandfather's father farmed Great Law, the next

---

[1] A shed for cattle or sheep.
[2] The wooden tub in which clothes are washed and beaten.

farm to Kidlaw, and they made a great deal of butter and cheese, and it was all salted butter, sold in butter firkins." [1] Miss Shanks thinks the butter firkins were new every time, but is not sure. Her grandfather farmed Kidlaw, three or four miles to the south.

Mrs. Hepple speaks of the cooper at Cambo who made butter firkins.

" Another reason for coopers was that the large houses made their own ale. They did at Wallington in Sir John Trevelyan's time, so the cooper had all these casks to repair and at other seasons he mended tubs, and made butter barrels.—Mrs. Keith.

" The malt was dried at the malt kil' at Rothley, but not in my time nor my father's, but in his people's perhaps. At the beginning of my time they had a beautiful wooden spade to turn the barley."—Mrs. Pearson, who lived in " the malt kil'." Her father's aunt, who lived with them, was born in 1777. The father came to Rothley to live with this aunt.

We know from a story told by Mr. Isaac Perceval, retired gamekeeper, Angerton Mill, aged seventy-eight, that the ale was brewed at Wallington in Isaac Milburn's day, that is about 1829.

Lime.

" Before they had lime kil's, they used to burn the lime on the ground by the side of the road, and you can see the place yet near Rothley East Shiel.[2] My great-grandfather used to burn the lime. He lived in one of two cottages called Clayton's Cottages, which used to be near Rothley East Shiel. Bowie was alive when I came here first, he lived in the next cottage to my great-grandfather and could tell me about him. Bowie died thirty years ago; he was seventy when he died."—Mr. William Embleton, carter, Dovecot.

Claypits.

Mr. George Handyside was asked about the hollows at the west side of his field near " the north road ":

[1] Small barrels.
[2] The holes he refers to where the lime was burnt are very large deep ones,—both round and square.

" They were clay pits; they made bricks and tiles there. They still get clay from them for puddling,—blue clay. The man that had the public-house, no, not Mr. Arthur—before him—had the field, and he used to try and plough in the holes, and his ploughs were for ever at the blacksmith's. It was long before my time." [1]

Mr. Edward Keith writes:—" The bricks for the Wallington Garden walls were said to be manufactured here by Sir Walter Blackett in the middle of the eighteenth century."

Lead Mines.

" There were lead mines near Fallowlees Burn to the left, when going to Fallowlees from Greenleighton."—Mr. George Handyside.[2]

Quarries at Greenleighton.

" There used to be two farms at Greenleighton, a lot of people lived there. There is whinstone, limestone and free-stone in the quarries there; it's the Ratcheugh—the whin dyke that runs right across the country."—Mr. George Handyside.

His uncle, Mr. George Richardson, who farmed Broom House long ago, was a great geologist and taught him both geology and farming.

" There were gannister[3] quarries. There used to be a graveyard at Greenleighton."—Miss McCracken. Her father farmed it years ago, and she lived there.

Coal Pits.

" There was a colliery in the ' Pit Field ' [at Cambo]; yes, where the beast fell in three or four years ago. Aye, and the drift runs down from there to the Wansbeck, and there's a stone in the wood to the west of Wallington, saying here's where the seam ends, and the drift begins. The seam runs right down there. There is coal everywhere, only it is a thin strata. There is good coal to the west of Wallington." —Mr. George Handyside.

[1] The public-house came to an end as long ago as 1862.
[2] Hodgson, II. 1, p. 289.
[3] A close grained sandstone.

It was an eighteenth century colliery. (Hodgson, II. 1, p. 276.)

" There was a colliery at the Saugh House, yes, in one of Mr. Henderson's fields. I can mind when that one was worked. There were four cottages at the Saugh House, where the men lived who worked in the colliery. All these cottages have gone now. Aye, there was one cottage in your backyard, and one at the Saugh House which is a byre[1] now, and two or three at Elf Hills. There were one or more cottages at all the farms then."—Mr. George Handyside.

" There were three cottages at the Lower Saugh House, which was in the wood below Miss McCracken's."—Mr. George Charlton.

Tailors and Schoolmasters on the Fells[2]

" My grandfather was a tailor at Rothley; he lived in the old malt kil', there were three or four families lived in it. In those days tailors went out to work; we stayed at the farm-houses maybees a week at a time till our work was finished. When I was first apprenticed I was about thirteen, and they gave me the lap-board and the irons to carry. There was one place out on the fells where we stayed a week— Chartners, three miles beyond Greenleighton. There were three daughters there. It was that dark at night that we were afeard to go out. One night it was pitch dark, and you couldn't see your hand before your face; it was *three miles* to Greenleighton, and one of the daughters walked there! The hedge schoolmaster was at Chartners,—but ye'll not know what a hedge schoolmaster is,—he went out and held school first in one farmhouse, then in another.[3]

When she came in she said to him, ' Maister, it *was* dark, I verra' near lost mysel',' and he said, ' I thocht ye were gey daft[4] to go out sic a night.'

I knew another schoolmaster who made his living partly by making baskets.

My grandfather served his time as a tailor at Blackcock

---

[1] A cowshed.
[2] Moors and wild hilly country.
[3] Staying there as the tailors did for days at a time.
[4] " Very foolish."

Hall, and the man he served his time with, said it was ' in the midst o' my work ! ' There was more population up there then, a good few worked at the lead mines at Fallowlees, and there was a colliery near the road to Rothbury then, near Coldrife and Birkheadsmoor on the right hand side before you get to the public-house on the left hand side. We got our coals there."—Mr. George Handyside.

" Blackcock Hall at the foot of Simonside. There used to be nine tailors there."—Miss McCracken.

" My father's aunt was a *dressmaker*, and used to go out to the farmhouses for a month at a time, dressmaking, quilting, patching.[1]

My father was a tailor in a small way, he had one man, and kept cotton, and linen and cloth; he and old Mr. Handyside were good friends, and when Mr. Handyside was busy he would help him, and when my father was busy Mr. Handyside would take some of the work to sew for him. Sometimes there would be a big funeral order. There were no sewing machines, it was all done by hand, and my father was specially famous for his buttonholes. I think he served his time at Long Witton.

My brother-in-law, George Thornton, was at school at Greenleighton in a cottage there; the master, Mr. Brown, was a besom maker, and he used to make besoms all the time they were doing their lessons, but he made them do them. He would make a chain, too, out of wood just with his penknife." (Mrs. Pearson showed one, skilfully made.) " He made baskets too. I'll lend you the poems Thornton wrote about Cambo in the old days. He was a wonderful man, Thornton; he made a fiddle, and he taught himself to read music, and he could play although he had no ear. Yes, he made a bicycle and a tricycle."—Mrs. Pearson.

The following poem on Greenleighton and its tiny school is given here with Mrs. Thornton's kind permission.

[1] See p. 70 for statement about earnings.
Mrs. Pearson still has her great-aunt's spectacles with her name, Hannah Robson, scratched on the metal. They are a very old-fashioned shape with tiny glasses.

My Birthplace

Greenleighton, place where I was born,
And spent with joy life's early morn,
 Thy scenes to me were fair:
To stranger eye thy charms are few,
Thy landscapes tame, but to my view
 None with them could compare.

What lovely spots my childhood found,
And gave me joy to sport around,
 And deem'd them most complete.
How glad when Spring returned again,
I heard with joy the green lap-wing
 Its pee-wit call repeat.

The curlew, too, whose welcome voice,
Returning, made my heart rejoice,
 The screaming tarry too:[1]
I also hailed another pledge,
That Winter's snows and storms had fledg'd,
 And bade us all adieu.

The cawing rooks I watched with glee,
Building their nests high on the tree,
 And noisy trow were they,
How they did steal and disagree!
And oh, what thieves they proved to be,
 And carried sticks away,

From off the nests their neighbours made;
They were not slow, homes to invade,
 If owners absent were;
And havoc make to such extent,
That much good time again was spent
 The building to repair.

And Summer, too, her charms did bring,
The soaring lark, his song did sing
 In heavenly precincts nigh.
The fleecy flock were then to lave,
To plunge into the cleansing wave,
 And soon as they were dry,

---

[1] Perhaps an allusion to the black-headed gulls which nest now not far off at Fallowlees.

Their woolly coats were off them shorn
By stalwart herds—outlandish born,
   Full of life and merry.
These busy times gave childhood joy;
No toil was it, when found employ,
   The tarry brand to carry.
And then when hay-time did begin.
No toil was it to assist in
   The ten o'clocks to bear:
Where lusty men, with sweeping blades,
The grass did cut, and lay in swathes,
   To win and wither there.

'Twas grand to see, six men or more,
In sweeping, measured strokes that bore
   Ten feet of grass away!
By eighteen inches with each slash,
And should there be one over rash,
   Disorder then held sway!
And then when Autumn's browning sun
Its work of rip'ning crops had done,
   And harvest gathered in,
What gave me joy was then to see
The wild geese flocks then wont to flee,
   As night was closing in,

Across the sky of sober grey
From stubble fields—where during day
   They gleaning there had been—
To lodge the night at Fallow lees,
In lonely loch securely,
   To eye of man unseen.
It was the cadence of their call,
Like music sweet on ear did fall,
   That signall'd their approach.
This 'bout a month was nightly heard
Across the Moorland wild and hard,
   As they on loch encroach.

But not so now—scarce ever heard
Or seen is now this noble bird,
   So common in those days;
And how it comes I cannot tell,
This visitor to loch on fell,
   Should change so much its ways.

And then, when Winter bleak was seen,
Stalking in white upon the scene,
   He too e'en had a charm.
When o'er high Simonside came he,
Enwrapped in drifts capriciously,
   Riding upon the storm.

Here too did stand the district school,
Whose humble walls enclosed no rule
   From Government Inspectors;
The masters old, the scholars few,
The code here taught was nothing due
   To any school directors.

To read and write, and cypher well,—
'Bout grammar he had nought to tell,
   Geography or hist'ry!
He well could make a grey goose quill,
And use it he could better still,
   He could write excellently!

And besoms make the very best;
He sold them East, he sold them West,
   And always had demand!
And " swills " [1] he made; they were as good
As hands could make with willow wood,
   And soon were off his hand!

And well he could the graver use,
Engrave your name on what you choose,
   On silver, watch or spoon;
A walking-stick he well could trim,
Could gloss it up and make it prim,
   Yes, neatly done and soon.

The pocket knife—his fav'rite tool—
He well could use, and in the school
   Did wondrous things produce,
As wooden chains, with swivels form'd
From solid wood, and well adorn'd
   With carving rich and choice.

[1] A swill is " a round basket of unpeeled willows."

'Twas just an old deserted house,
The roof was thatch, grey as a mouse,
   The school of which I sing;
But what of that?—our tasks were light,
When day was done, no work at night!
   In play we had full swing.

And if we no inspections had
To rack our brains and make us sad,
   Like scholars nowadays.
We had no treats to make us smile,
No railway trips to sea awhile,
   To view the rolling waves.

Few holidays had we to spend,
On Saturdays we did attend
   From morn till sunny noon.
" Lay by your books! " was promptly met,
Our hats we seized, the school we left,
   'Twas ours the afternoon!

In retrospect I ask, oh where
Are all my schoolmates gone—oh where?
   An echo answers where?
Thirteen I know have quit life's scene,
And are as if they had not been,
   As to this world of care.

But still the world retains their dust,
A charge to keep—a sacred trust,
   Until the time shall come
When Christ the Lord, His own shall call;
If any are the Lord's they shall
   Arise—then wafted Home!

Lines written by George Thornton, Star View, Rothbury, formerly of Ewesley Station. In memoriam paper printed by Northern Counties Bible Tract Depot, and reprinted with their consent.

" Mr. Codling used to say the last schoolmaster of Greenleighton village made beehives (straw skeps) when teaching—one a day. He knew the day of the week by the number."— Mr. Edward Keith.

There was a schoolmaster at Donkin Rig of the name of Brown; he lived at the Saugh House afterwards; he carved walking sticks, and mended sieves. My father remembers taking a riddle to him to mend."—Miss Murray.

" The schoolmaster at Donkin Ridge used to go about from place to place. The old school is a hemmel now. During the last years previous to West Rothley School being built, the Donkin Ridge one was probably permanent.

When I was first at West Rothley School post was never delivered, we had to fetch it from Rothley; once in a snowstorm I walked to fetch it *on the walls*, and it took me all the afternoon, and I brought back everybody's letters for the last week. Then they started deliveries three times a week."—Miss Richardson, once schoolmistress at West Rothley.

" I used to know a *schoolmaster* close to Forestburn Gate station " (three stations north of Scots Gap); " he kept school in a cottage—only had seven children. No, *he* didn't make baskets, the farmers on the fells were good to him, and when he wasn't teaching he was at the public-house. I used to meet him on the road in a long hat, and a coat with swallow tails; sometimes he came back, and sometimes he didn't. He was a good crack,[1] and he'd keep them entertained all night. A very far larned man he was. He made some fine scholars in Rothbury Forest."—Mr. Isaac Perceval.

Miss Richardson has charge of a manuscript list of scholars attending Cambo school, 1784-1805, made out by the retiring master, William Robson. The rhymes therein have already been printed in a book or books about this neighbourhood (see Tomlinson, " Guide to Northumberland," p. 260), so are not repeated here. But the list is interesting, showing how many of the old families are still represented in and round Cambo. Mr. Robson undertook to teach the following special subjects, and did so in many cases: —

Mensuration, book-keeping, trigonometry, surveying of land, dialling, gauging, navigation, algebra.

Quilting was also at one time done by men. " Joe the Twilter " was a well-known character on Tyneside, who was murdered in his house, near Warden, because he was supposed to be well off.

Mr. R. Adam Wilson knew him well.

[1] Brocket (1846 edition) defines " crack " as " chat, conversation, news."

FROM PACK-HORSES TO RAILWAYS

The Pack-Horses.

" My eldest brother, who is joiner with Lord Scarborough at Lumley Castle, heard far more from Grannie than any of us, and he says that that old thatched cottage[1] was a beer-house in the days when the pack-horses travelled. Just to the west of the cottage there is a road through the belt of trees—you can tell where it's been—that is the way they travelled. In front of the house was a duck pond, and Grand-father made the garden both back and front. Mr. Clennell of Harbottle supplied him with most of his flowers and apple trees."—Dictated by Mrs. Hedley, and her daughter—Miss Hilda Hedley; it is Mrs. Hedley's brother, Mr. William Pearson, who is referred to. He is sixty-four years of age. Mrs. Hedley remembers that " the field behind Benty was ploughed," which accounts for there being little sign of a road beyond the belt of trees to the west.

Mr. Robert Armstrong, joiner, Cambo, thinks it would be the plantation itself which was the pack-road, and was after-wards planted. It is just the width of pack-roads, he knows in other parts of the country. But if so, he says, it must have been a long time ago, on account of the size of the oaks.

Mr. Edward Keith writes:—" This was one of the main pack-roads leading north from Cambo, previous to Sir Walter Blackett building the straight carriage road from Wallington to Harwood Cottages. Probably, the beeches were planted about the time it ceased to be used. Pearson didn't take up his residence there until the first quarter of the nineteenth century."

Coaching.

" The old coaching road used to run past your house [in Cambo] to Elsdon, and " The Chevy Chase " used to change horses at your house which was the old inn. The road was not quite the same as now; as you go down to Elsdon you can see where the old road went; it just avoided Elsdon, but it was an awkward hill, and they changed it.

---

[1] The cottage is now pulled down, but the site is still affectionately spoken of as " Black Benty." See Chapter XVI, pp. 116, 117, for story of " Andra Pearson," the " grandfather," who lived here.

Then a Company was formed, which made " the New Line " [that is the new road], from Belsay to Otterburn, but unfortunately for them Stephenson invented the steam engine, and the railway was made just about the time the New Line became the coaching road. They had a toll gate at Belsay and at Knowesgate.

The old men used to tell us, that one reason the coaching road was changed was because of an accident, close to Wallington gates, where there is a sharp corner, and the coach turned right over. They were allowed after that to move the wall back, and you can see where they did it, by the stump of a tree, left just outside the wall, between Graham's house and the corner.

After the New Line was opened, they changed horses at Kirkwhelpington (at what is now Miss Moffat's boarding-house), and at Raylees, but the inn at Kirkwhelpington was so awkward to reach [on account of the very steep hill], that they did not take the coach there, only the horses."—Mr. Edward Keith.

One of the contractors for the New Line was known as " Ready Money Joe," because he used to pay his men every week. They didn't all do that!—Mr. George Handyside.

" My uncle, who lived at Shillaw Hill, has come by coach along that road [from the Gibbet past Harwood Gate]. My grandfather farmed Shillaw Hill. My uncle used to get his horses done at that blacksmith's shop." [1]—Mrs. Davison, Low Fairnley.

The Inn at Cambo, to which Mr. Keith has referred,[2] and which Mr. George Thornton's poem described,[3] ceased to be a public-house in the time of Sir Walter Trevelyan, and after being a Temperance Hotel for a few years it became the agent's house and afterwards the house of Eleanora, Lady Trevelyan, Sir Charles's widow, until her death in 1919.

" Rutherford was the last to have it as a public-house, and he had it also for a year or two as a temperance hotel. We came to live here[4] sixty years ago, that is in 1862, I remember

---

[1] The one there used to be between the Gibbet and Harwood Gate. See Chapter XXVII, p. 180.

[2] Page 54.

[3] Page 43.

[4] That is in the inn. The conversation was in his old home.

getting out of the cart at the door, and we were here five years, so the sign must have been taken down in 1867."—Mr. John Henderson, Temperance Hotel, Scots Gap, to which they moved in 1867.

He also states that the old dogwheel[1] used to be in " the front kitchen," fixed up on the wall in a recess to the north of the fireplace. It was not used. The " front kitchen " was the front room to the east of the front door; there was a glass partition from the door to near the window, and that was where they kept the drink.[2]

The old sign was taken down to Wallington when the inn became the agent's house, but was lent to the present occupiers, Miss J. D. Carr and Miss R. E. Bosanquet, by Sir George and Lady Trevelyan, and hangs in the house.

" They were just called Queen Mary and Queen Elizabeth. Many a snowball I've given her (Elizabeth), yes, she got it the worst, she looked to the south. They *were* done up once, I can't mind who by. The Beaumonts were the best painters; they were in Morpeth. They were sent for to London once. Portraits and house decorating. Yes, I can mind the last of them. Miss Taylor's mother was one of them, and Mrs. Garvey of Rothbury was another. One of the Garveys is an artist now."—Mr. George Charlton.

Miss Gow, who used to live in the house, believes the sign was painted by Pauline, Lady Trevelyan, and by Miss Lofft, afterwards Lady Trevelyan, Sir Walter's second wife. The one did Mary, the other Elizabeth.[3]

The Name of the Inn.

Mrs. Hepple of Rugley Walls says her husband, Mr. Thomas Hepple, always told her it was " the Two Queens." This is confirmed by Murray's " Handbook for Northumberland and Durham," edition of 1860.

Mr. Edward Keith thinks the old men called it " the Rival Queens."

After the coaching days were past Sir Walter Trevelyan kept a pair of post-horses for hiring out. Bella Stokoe, who

---

[1] By which a dog once turned the spit with meat before the fire.

[2] The dogwheel is now preserved in the present kitchen at the back of the house.

[3] Other people say that the painting is not of so recent a period. Pauline, Lady Trevelyan, was a friend of Ruskin's.

used to live in what is now " the wash-house," was wife of the post-boy.—Mr. John Henderson.

The road used to come right up to the inn.—Mr. George Charlton.

Riding.

The farmers' daughters used to ride to market, so Miss Richardson tells us. She has a letter from an old cousin relating how " eerie his mother felt riding home alone in the dusk of the evening after accidentally witnessing the procession to the last Berwick execution." This seems to refer to a date between 1820 and 1840.

Old Andra Pearson,—Peninsular veteran, mole-catcher, weaver and gardener, born in 1789, " used to ride about on a large white donkey," says his great-granddaughter, Miss Hilda Hedley.[1]

Johnnie Anderson, mason, and owner of fighting cocks,[2] used to ride " a large brown donkey. Donkeys were much larger in those days. He would ride it all the way to Rothbury races and back."—Mr. Walter Hedley.

" They would go so fast! "—Mrs. Hedley.

Carriers.

" My father's great-grandfather was a Scotch carrier from Scotland to Newcastle; it was a Scotch name. They were queer roads; afterwards they made the New Line. He used to stop the night at Raylees, on the road from Carter Bar. Raylees was a public-house then.[3]

We only had the papers once a week; the carrier used to bring them from Newcastle. He lived at Rothley. He had a very old horse, and my mother came out one day, and said to him, ' Thou ought to get thyself a new horse, Jimmy! ' ' I'll get mysel' an Iron Horse, next week! ' but he never did." [4] Mr. George Handyside. His grandfather was the

---

[1] See also Chapter XVI, pp. 116, 117.

[2] See also Chapter IV, pp. 71-72.

[3] He must have come by the old drove road, which is marked out with stones near Raylees, nine miles or so from Cambo. It is now only a farm, but the fact that there is an ice-house shows it was once a place of some importance.

[4] Compare Mackenzie's " Northumberland," published 1825. " A curious, self-moving machine, called an Iron Horse, erected a few years

Mr. T. Richardson, referred to by Hodgson, in his " History of Northumberland," published 1827, II. 1, p. 281.

" Cambo was a very busy place then, I've seen five or six carriers carts loused[1] up yonder; they came from up Redes-dale, and sometimes stopped the night at the ' Highlander,' [2] or somewhere, and went on to Newcastle. The railway put a stop to all that."—Mr. George Charlton.

The Railway.

" When it was decided to make the railway there was great rejoicing, the children had a holiday, and there was a *dance* in the barn at Cambo. And when the railway was opened the children and old people many of them went by train from Cambo to Middleton,[3] and back by the next train. And I was amongst them. There was a dance behind the public-house at Middleton."—Mrs. Thomas Hepple.

" Grandmother was never in a train, but she never missed seeing the train go by, she used to go out with her stick at Benty."—Miss Hilda Hedley, speaking of her great-grand-mother, the wife of Andra Pearson, the Peninsular veteran.

The railway was opened about the time Mrs. Henderson, Mr. John Henderson's mother, came to Cambo, in 1862.

The Reedsmouth line was made first, the line to Rothbury from Scots Gap Junction was made later.

Mr. William Embleton has also reckoned back that it is " fifty-eight or sixty years since the railway was started from Reedsmouth to Scots Gap, over fifty-eight years." [4]

Miss McCracken says " we came to Northumberland in 1869, and it was not quite new then. The train on the Reedsmouth line had the reputation of stopping to let you gather mushrooms, certainly it used to stop to pick up Mr. McCracken, near Blackhall."

Miss J. D. Carr says that she always heard the same thing

ago . . . at Newbottle Colliery with legs to assist its ascent, and to retard its descent . . . the boiler burst, and several lives being lost, the invention was abandoned." Vol. I, p. 148 note.

[1] Loosed, unyoked.

[2] The " Highlander " is a public-house on the road between Belsay and Newcastle.

[3] The next station on the way to Morpeth.

[4] That is since they started making it.

about the train on the Rothbury line, as regards mushroom gathering.

Line from Scots Gap to Rothbury.

It was stated at an Institute Meeting that Sir Walter Trevelyan was very anxious for the railway to be made, and that quarries and limekilns were started, in order to make traffic for the railway.

In 1875 there was a railway accident, not very far from Scots Gap Station. Four people were killed. " My father and Uncle Joe were in the railway accident, it was near Donkin Ridge. Jack[1] was in it too, but he wasn't hurt. My father never worked again. The carriages got separated, and went over the embankment. They [her relatives] had just finished re-building Rothley Lake House, and they had all their tools with them; they never saw them again. One of their labourers, Fenwick, was killed, and another, Tulip, was badly hurt."—Mrs. Armstrong.

Mrs. Armstrong has a cutting from a newspaper printed two days later. Amongst the list of injured are:—

> Joseph Robinson, builder, Scots Gap.
> Robert Robinson, mason, Scots Gap.
> Henry Codling, joiner, Wallington.

The newspaper account explains that there were eight stone wagons on the same train with passengers. The line had been " formed a few years ago by an independent company, consisting of landowners of the locality, and other gentlemen . . . with the hope . . . of its ultimately forming part of a central through line between Edinburgh and London. The project was, in the first instance, to carry the line through from Scots Gap to Cornhill, but . . . through want of capital " and support it was never taken beyond Rothbury. " Since the advent of the railway, capital has been directed to the working of coal, lime, fireclay and stone for building purposes." About twelve months after its opening it was sold to the North British Railway Company.

In a little book of printed poems by Hannah R. Brown, Rothley, there is one on this accident.

Both the poem and the newspaper account speak with

---

[1] Her brother, Mr. Robinson, builder, Cambo.

appreciation of the services rendered to the injured by the Misses Winship, whose father farmed Kirkhill; they were in an adjoining field when the accident took place.

HOME LIFE

Houses.

We were talking about Peter Brice, the baker, and wondering why there had been a baker in old days in Cambo, whereas now there is no baker; loaves can only be bought from a van from Morpeth once a week, with yeast and sausages, and we all bake at home.

Mr. Isaac Perceval explained:—

" There was a time about ninety years ago when there were *no ovens and no windows;* when people shifted they had to take their windows and their fireplaces with them.

No, the houses *weren't* all alike, the windows were different sizes, and they had to be made right with boards,— and with cow dung. I've seen a house myself where you went in here, and there was the cow, and here was the cuddy,[1] and the living-room was there " (" And the hens would be in the passage," put in his housekeeper). " I've been there often, for my grandfather was born there." [You had to pass through the byre, past the heels of the cow and the cuddy to reach the living-room.] He described another house in Angerton, which stood where the joiner's shop now is, where a family of at least seven children had been brought up by their parents long ago. It consisted of one room.

Another speaker, referring to about the year 1870, in the neighbourhood we are dealing with, said the houses were hovels, the pig would be underneath,—in the cellar.

Mr. George Handyside can remember when the back row at Cambo was all black thatch, and when there was at least one house where the cow and the people went in and out by the same door. " I've seen a lot of changes."

" I remember grand the last house I was in when they moved the hearthstones, the fourth house in the back row; Tom Wilson, when he moved, took the hearthstones and everything with him."—Mr. William Pearson. Repeated and dictated by Mrs. Hedley, and Miss Hilda Hedley.

[1] Donkey.

Mrs. Pearson says they always had an oven, but it was very small, and she *has* seen bread baked in the pot, —— did it, afterwards they gave her a wee oven.

" When we came from Scotland in 1869, we brought all our own fireplaces with us."—Miss McCracken.

" My mother says when she was young they always took the fire stones with them. And they had no ovens, and cooked the bread in the pot."—Miss Murray.

" Yes, and they roasted the meat, and made porridge in yettlins[1] too, and put red hot coals on the top of the lid."—Miss McCracken.

Mr. R. Adam Wilson, butcher and farmer, New Houses, Capheaton, confirms the statement about the ovens. The oven and pot at Clock Mill belonged to his uncle.

Mr. James Wilkinson of Hartington can remember when " there were middens in front of the houses at Cambo, but Sir Charles[2] wouldn't have it, and made the gardens. He made the extra room to our house. He not only gave the orders, and found out what was needed, but saw that it was done."

Mrs. Pearson, has given the following description of the house at Rothley Village where she lived as a child:—
" It was called the Malt Kil', they dried the barley on the top floor, and we lived on the floor below; there were two rooms on the ground floor, and two rooms on the first floor, and attics above, where they dried the barley. The walls were three feet thick, and there was a great iron bar across it, to keep it together; some of Sir Walter's men put it in the attics and you had to step over it. No, I never heard it was a pele tower." [3]

---

[1] Three-legged pots.

[2] Sir Charles Trevelyan, born 1807, inherited Wallington from his cousin, Sir Walter, in 1879; died 1886.

[3] The Editor was inclined to think the malt kil' might have been a pele tower, but Mr. John Henderson says it was not strong enough. Probably it was " the old hall, which is of three stories, and was once a residence of a branch of the Carnaby family." Hodgson, II. 1, p. 307.

We all fed pigs; and salted them upstairs; and all the coals were to be carried upstairs in big swills.[1]—Mrs. Pearson.

Miss Richardson tells us that when she used to visit Mrs. Waitte, at Harwood House, on the moor, there was a *canvas ceiling;* probably the house wasn't ceiled. It has since been pulled down.   There was a canvas ceiling in a house at Rothley too.

In an old house at Harnham, near Belsay, occupied by Miss Wake, there is a fixed cupboard bed under the stairs in one of the sitting-rooms. The tradition is that the panels of the cupboard were painted by Thomas Whittell,[2] poet, painter and sundial maker who died in 1736.   There are festoons of leaves and apples, a canopy and curtains, and little conventional trees, suggestive of an Italian altar piece, with the Madonna and Child left out.   It raises the question whether any Italian workmen could have started on alterations at Wallington, and given ideas to Whittell before he died, but 1736 seems rather too early for them.   At the head and foot of the bed are shelves.   The old treasures in this house have been wonderfully preserved, partly owing to the fact that the Misses Leighton, to whose family it belonged, lived to a great age, the last one dying twelve years ago at ninety-three years of age; and Miss Wake had lived with them.   There is an old *jack* in the kitchen for roasting the meat.

The *Handicrafts* of sixty or seventy years ago can also be seen,—wax flowers delicately modelled, and coloured, evidently direct from nature, laburnum and water-lily, snowdrops, convolvulus, and many others, even the stamens touched with the right colour; the Misses Leighton's brother was very fond of flowers, and could give them any flower they wanted, Miss Wake says.   There is a picture frame in *leather,* decorated with leaves, acorns and tree flowers finely made in leather, which reminds us of Institute leather work to-day.

" We only had one room, and there were seven of us children.   It was a large room, and we had two four-pole beds, and a desk bed, and *a hauly bed* on castors that you pulled out from under a four-pole bed, and three of us children were put to sleep in it.   Later, we had two rooms.

---

[1] Large open baskets.
[2] Compare Chapter XI, p. 105.

In those days, my father had to pay *sixpence a week for schooling* for each of us, and had to pay for everything we used, pens, ink, and books. It was threepence a week for labourers' children, but he was a mechanic."—Mrs. Pearson.

" Closed beds, box beds, or cupboard beds were common, until twenty or thirty years ago in Northumberland. In my childhood, forty years ago, almost every hind's kitchen had two box beds, filling up one wall of the room entirely; in still older times, they had doors, which could be closed. On the beds were fine patchwork quilts, or beautiful quilts, quilted with long flowing patterns, such as are still made at home."—Rosalie E. Bosanquet.

Sometimes there was a bed underneath, " which could be pulled out like a drawer."—Mrs. William Wilson.

" *Chaff Beds* were greatly used, within the memory of many of us. They were very comfortable and clean, for the ticks were washed and filled again, nearly every year, after the thresher had been. But they have gone out now."—Miss Richardson, Mrs. Thomas Hepple, Mrs. Robert Hepple.

The *Grey Stone Slates* which were so much used for roofing buildings here, were put together formerly with sheep bones, Mrs. Charles Trevelyan reminds us.

Mr. George Charlton confirms this; they used to be put together with sheep shank[1] bones, more recently with wooden or iron pegs. The stone slates are heavy, and are not put on new buildings now.

" My grandfather was a slater, and I've seen him splitting the sheep bones in winter for fastening the slates together, afterwards they used wood, preparing it also in the winter."— Mr. John Robinson.

Spinning.

" When we were children, we were sent out to gather wool, when we came home from school, and it was—who would get a bagful first. In the evening, we would have to pick the motes out of the wool, we didn't like that. Then, it was sent to Otterburn mills, and carded, and then, my mother spun it on her big wheel—wool for stockings. She had two spinning wheels, the little one for spinning linen, the big one for spinning wool. If it was for stockings, she

[1] Leg.

twisted it herself, and knitted it. If it was for blankets, it went back to Otterburn to be woven." Mrs. Thomas Hepple had one of her mother's blankets, till quite lately.

Mrs. Robert Hepple adds, that they still send wool to Otterburn, and have it made up into blankets and bed rugs. The less good wool can be made into bed rugs.

It was the usual custom, for all the country women, to go out early in the morning, say four a.m., to gather wool from the hedges; they had to go early, because the tramps and muggers[1] would have been before them. They would get a bag full of wool, and take it to the mills at Otterburn,[2] or at Netherwitton, to be prepared for them to spin into yarn. " My mother, Mrs. Hedley of Horncastle, Kirkwhelpington, used to go out, and she had two spinning wheels, one large, one small." After being spun, it was taken back to the mills, to be made into a couple of blankets, or enough tweed to make a suit for the husband. It is when the sheep get poor that they lose great quantities of wool.—Mrs. Truelove.

Mrs. Thomas Hepple has heard her mother say that, " when she was in service, they used to spin a lot of linen, for the men's shirts, every winter, and also yarn for cloth, for men's suits, and also wool for carpets. I've heard her tell, how they were stinted[3] to a certain amount, and, if they hadn't got it done, they had to sit up, till it was done." [4]

(Her mother, Mrs. Kell, died twenty-five years ago, in her one hundred and second year.)

Her mother bought her lint, but she cannot say where. She never heard of it being grown in these parts. She spun it on her little spinning wheel. When things got cheaper, and she did not need her spinning wheel, Mr. Perceval of Long Witton bought the little one.

An old Mrs. Codling, at the Dovecot, had a great deal of spun lint, it had been spun by her daughter-in-law, and, at her sale, Mrs. Hepple bought it, and had it made into sheets.

---

[1] Hawkers of mugs, earthenware, etc.

[2] The Otterburn mills are very old ones, and are a feature of the countryside; the farmers still send their wool, and get it back as blankets, or tweed as required.

[3] " Stint . . . a piece of work to be accomplished within a given time."—Heslop, " Northumberland Words."

[4] Dictated by Mrs. T. Hepple.

She showed a skein of spun lint, which she had kept as a curiosity, and also a piece of lint before it was spun (brown in colour).

At our Treasure Evening Mrs. Robert Wilson showed " Adam's shirt, seventy years old. Given to me for Adam by his grandmother. It was spun by his great-great-grand-mother, made by his great-grandmother. Worn by his grandfather, and his father, and himself." It is neatly marked, R.A.W., in fine cross stitch, with a flower under-neath—his grandfather's initials and his own—and is made of fine linen. It is the size for a small boy, and this last Adam has outgrown it.—Mrs. Robert Wilson.

Dress.

At an Institute Meeting, Mrs. Keith showed a dainty *silver knee buckle*, which had belonged to an ancestor of hers,—John Codling, who was clerk for sixty years at Kirk-whelpington; for further particulars about him, and his building of the so-called Percy Cross at Otterburn, she refers us to Hodgson's History.[1] His dress was *blue breeches, silk stockings, and cut away coat*. The buckle was given to her as a child by an old relation, " and when I brought it home, I was told to take it back, as it ought not to be separated from the other, but the old lady said, " I'll give it where I please."

" I can see Sir Walter [Trevelyan] as he used to come into the school; he always wore a *plaid*; the men did then instead of the coats they wear now. The men used to wear *brocade waistcoats* with nice buttons, and *white shirts* with *ruffles* and *long hats*. They would never have thought of wearing striped or dark shirts as they do now. Was this your father's waistcoat, or mine? " Mrs. Hedley asked her husband, showing a beautiful bright blue, brocade waistcoat, edged with leather, and small buttons covered with the same brocade. " The women wore a cap after they were married, my mother didn't like it, and never did it."

Mrs. Hepple and Miss Shipley have two *fine silk and crêpe shawls*, which belonged to their mother. Mrs. Hepple

---

[1] Hodgson, II. 1, p. 207. John Codling, parish clerk, buried 1826, aged seventy-nine, " clerk for sixty-three years " except for short intervals of ill-health, or absence for work.

E

remembers her wearing the largest one with iridescent colouring, and she used to tell her, that she had worn it originally with a spencer, and a white skirt, very narrow, with a frill at the bottom, and embroidered. Mrs. Hepple made the white skirt into a christening robe for a grandchild.

The women workers, on the farms, used to wear large shady bonnets for their work, which were called " uglies." They were quite different from any sunbonnet worn now, for the part, which shaded the face, was held out by four or five canes. The Cambo women all used to wear them for the haymaking, in Sir Walter's time. Then clouty bonnets —sunbonnets—came in.—Mrs. Hedley.

" The farmers used to go to market in long hats. When I first came here Mr. Thornton of Cornhills did so."—Miss Richardson.

Food and Candles.

" *Salt* was 5s. a stone! I've heard my mother say they used to clarify the salt of the water in which beef had been salted, and use it to salt the porridge! I've heard her tell that many a time. In places, where she was servant, they used to take the boxes of salt and *candles* up to the hills, to be safe from the exciseman."—Mrs. Thomas Hepple.

Her sister, Miss Shipley, put in, " I've dipped candles," and described the process—the tub with fat on the top, and boiling water underneath, " not much water."

Mrs. Thomas Hepple has two moulds for making candles, two candles in each. She made the candles of beef tallow, and set the moulds up in sand to cool.

Mrs. Bell, Broom House, Meldon, says that people used to fasten their shutters, when making their candles, as it was a Government monopoly.

The subject was discussed at an Institute Meeting, and it was said to be " dutiable." Miss McCracken told the story of a woman dipping candles; when word came " the gaugers are coming," she hid them in the manure heap, and they all melted,—but she got the *wicks* back! [This didn't happen at Cambo.]

They used to turn the kitchen table upside down, and put the candles into it to dry, after they had been dipped, as then the grease didn't show. And when they were dry they took them out in a box, and buried them.

Mrs. Robson, wife of the farmer at Broom House, Cambo, has a *candle-making machine;* it consists of half a dozen upright moulds, in each of which a wick is placed, the bottom plugged and the fat poured in. Mrs. Robson says it is worth doing if you kill your own sheep and have plenty of fat.

Her husband explained that the older method was to *dip* candles; for this, two long pieces of wood were set across the room, with wires between them, and the floor was covered with paper. There were nine or ten wicks hung from each wire; there was a large tub of fat, in which they had all to be dipped; when you had dipped them all once, you started again with the first one. They had to be dipped, perhaps a dozen times, till they got the required thickness. It was a rough day—candle-making.

Mrs. Robson's father, aged eighty-one, can remember the time when the windows were shuttered, and the doors barred, during candle-making, for fear of the gaugers.

Mr. Robson reminds us, that it was at about the same time, that windows were taxed, and windows were in consequence blocked up. He suggests that Troughend [near Otterburn] may be an instance of this.

It seems as if the women must have been very busy eighty years ago, when they had cows to attend to, and candle-making and spinning, besides cooking, and washing, and sewing; but Mrs. Robson reminds us that, in some ways, life was simpler, for instance, the floors were sanded.

Soap Making.

Mrs. Robson has made soap within the last few weeks:—

3 pints of water.
7 lbs. of fat.
1 lb. of caustic soda, which cost 1s. 4d.; and it made 12 lbs. of soap.

The caustic soda makes the water hot, put the fat in, stir it about, and set it in the kitchen in the inglenook to cool for twenty-four hours, then coup[1] it out of the pail, and keep it a month before using.

It is grand for cleaning clothes. The recipe was on the packet of caustic soda which she got from the chemist.

[1] Upset.

Food.

Mr. and Mrs. Robson say that *oatmeal* and *barley* are still included in the wages in Scotland. They themselves and their family are fond of *crowdy*, and of *barley bread*, and make them constantly. Crowdy is made of fine English oatmeal, with salt, and boiling water poured on to it. As for barley bread, they almost lived on it, during the war, as the meal was never adulterated.

" Highkil and Lowkil meal, used in the making of Porridge and Crowdy, are local names, given to the prepared meals, dried in the High Kiln, or the Low Kiln, in the old water-driven mills like Rothley."—Written down by Mrs. Keith.

Barley meal used to be given to beggars; " beggars' meal," it was called.—A member at Institute meeting.

Old Mortars and Creeing Stones.

There are many large stone receptacles, about two to two and a half feet in height, standing outside farmhouses, or in gardens, sometimes with plants growing in them, sometimes with a round stone on the top with a hole in it.

For instance there are three outside Hartington Hall. It is suggested that one of them was the font at the old chapel which there was once, close by, at Kirkhill. (There certainly is another stone, which seems to have been the capital of a pillar.) It has been suggested that they are cheese vats.

Mr. James Wilkinson, who has lived at Hartington all his life, thinks they have been for sheeling[1] barley, to make pearl barley, which was done with a round stone with a handle. These are rather higher than the usual type of mortar. Mr. Wilkinson adds, that the late Rev. C. A. Fitch thought the one, with more carving on it, must have been the font.

Miss Brown, at Newbiggin, has a mortar, with a round stone on the top, with a hole in the middle of it. She has been told, by an old lady, that it is a creeing stone.[2]

Mr. George Charlton says they usually have a hole for a handle, at the side, for turning them.

Mrs. Rutherford says that very large stones (like Miss

---

[1] " Sheel, to divest of the husk or shell. Sheel barley, barley shelled."—Heslop.

[2] " Creeing-trough . . . a large stone mortar used for creeing or taking off the husks of barley or wheat."—Brocket.

Brown's) with a hole hollowed out, were used for filtering water. She has lived chiefly in County Durham.

Her friend, Miss Shanks, Cambo, " had an uncle-in-law, who would be a good bit over a hundred, if he were alive now, who used to sheel barley in a mortar, with a stone on the top, with a hole in it; they put a stick through the hole," and worked it about.—Dictated by Miss Shanks.

Mr. Edward Keith writes :—" The flat mortars with the top rounded stones, and hole for handle, are querns,—old British hand mills. At a later date, when water mills superseded hand labour, they were often used for shelling barley, or bruising other products for domestic use."

We were discussing what people used to drink, when " tea was 7s. a lb.," [1] and Miss Ann Elizabeth Robson, Angerton Mill, told us about the *treacle beer* which her mother used to make,—treacle and lemon and ginger, and fermented with yeast (not black treacle); and about the *nettle beer* which she herself used to make :—

" Get the nettles young, and put them into the pan, and boil them; strain off into a vessel; put in whole ginger, take a hammer, break the ginger, and bruise it, and put in a couple of lemons sliced; when it's cooled, put in a slice of toasted bread,—crust is best with balm[2] spread on it; let it ferment three or four days, put your hand in, and lift the bread up, and throw it away with all the scum on it; put one and a half pounds of brown sugar in, strain it, let it cool and bottle it. And when you uncork it take care it does not wash you ! "
—Recipe dictated by Miss Robson.

" The shepherd's wife at Greenleighton used to make nettle beer."—Miss McCracken.

Miss Gow has mentioned *dandelion beer*.

" My mother always used to make her own *yeast*. She took hops and taties, and then she had an onset,[3] or got a mugful from some one who had some left over, and put it in, and bottled it off in stone bottles, and tied down the cork. Glass bottles would have broken."—Mr. Isaac Perceval.

[1] See also p. 70 for price of tea.
[2] Yeast.
[3] " A small portion of yeast retained to furnish a fresh fermentation."
—Heslop.

Miss Charlton's mother used to make it, when Miss Charlton was a child; one week she would make a setting, another week some one else would make it. " I've often been sent with a can for a setting."

Home Life on the North Tyne.

" To about the year 1850 rolling pins were not used to roll paste. The paste or dough was simply beaten on a board. White bread was almost unknown amongst the poorer classes, the flour being so expensive to buy. Barley cakes and porridge was the staple food as ovens were not in use; the scones were cooked on a girdle,[1] or on hot bricks. After being cooked, the cakes were placed on boards suspended from the rafters. Like flour, tea was almost prohibitive to the working classes on account of its cost, the price being then about 10s. per pound. It was only served out on Sundays. In a small village, it was the custom amongst the women, for each one to take her turn in making the tea and the neighbours assembled at her house to partake of the beverage, which no doubt would be very weak.

Comparing the *cost of labour* at the present day, to that of about eighty years ago, the usual charge for making a dress by a qualified *dressmaker* was 2s. and all the sewing was done by the hand. The needlework was very elaborate, rows and rows of tucks appearing on a dress. By working long hours a *tailor* was able to make the " handsome " sum of ninepence per day.

About the year 1780 my grandmother (Jean Thompson of Cranecleugh Farm) with her sisters walked every Sunday morning to Falstone Presbyterian Church, a distance of eight miles. In winter they rode on horseback. They wore homespun skirts either brown or green with loose bodices called Garibaldies, which are our present day jumpers. They wore white kerchiefs round the neck and instead of hats, huge poke bonnets were worn, some of which were very beautiful. Following the fashion of those days, they carried their stockings and shoon,[2] until they came to a small stream, about a mile from the church, where they washed their feet before putting on their shoon. Leather was very expensive

[1] A circular iron plate with a handle which is hung over the fire, and is still in constant use.
[2] Shoes.

in those days. Every morning and evening all the household assembled in the farm kitchen for prayers.

In my grandmother's time *box beds* were used; they were just like a huge box and had a moveable front. They were mostly all painted blue with green panels. Some of these beds are still to be seen far up in the Coquet district. When very cold at night the front of the bed was closed.—Mrs. Joseph Hall, written down by Miss Jessie Hall.[1]

COCKFIGHTING

" There was a cockpit in Wallington West Wood on a level place on a hill atwixt the Ice House Pond, and the Middle Pond. Benny Stott, who was eighty, was alive when I came here, and he told me.[2] There was one in the Cockplay plantation, near Scots Gap, but I don't know where.

There were two breeds, the dark ones, and the light ones. They were grand table birds, but they're hard to get now.

R—— C——, at Kirkwhelpington, had a lot of game cocks, walking them, on the farms, all over the moors.[3] They didn't do each other much harm when just fighting with the bare shanks[4] to see which was the best,—but when the long spurs were on,"—the speaker agreed it was rather brutal. " They fought them on the sly, after it was forbidden."—Mr. Walter Hedley.

" Johnnie Anderson and —— took their gamecocks to walk up on the fells. They would generally fight them in a room, in a public-house; Johnnie would get his out in a room, at Rothley, and put the nobs—dummies—on their spurs, so that they wouldn't hurt theirsel's, and then they'd spar a bit. They clipped their wings. It was Sundays they had the cock-fighting."—Mr. Isaac Perceval.

---

[1] The places mentioned and referred to in Mrs. Hall's contributions are quite outside our district, on the North Tyne, but I begged her to send them in as, owing to the great age to which her grandmother lived, she has direct knowledge of the facts, and they probably apply to our district also. Compare p. 35.

[2] Mr. Edward Keith writes:—" I knew old Ben Stott well forty years ago. He was then Head Forester at Wallington. He started as a Page, in Sir John Trevelyan's household, and used to tell, with glee, how he was horse-whipped, by the said Baronet, when he failed to preserve a menial's gravity at the dinner-table."

[3] In the same way as foxhound puppies are " walked."

[4] That is without the spurs.

" There is a ring on the knowe[1] yonder, it's about as big as this room; some people say that is where they had the cockfighting between Cambo and Kirkwhelpington." [2]— Mrs. Hedley, wife of farmer, Elf Hills.

" Old John Anderson used to keep a game cock and hen, and he used to take the cock to Morpeth, to fight.

I lived with my grandmother, at the inn at Netherwitton, and she had a cock to walk for a pitman;—and a man two houses away had one, and wanted to see them fight;—and the pitman's cock killed his!

When they hadn't good spurs, or when they were young, and their spurs were soft, they put on steel spurs,—strapped them on,—it was cruel. Johnnie Anderson bred them."— Mrs. Pearson.

" Many a time I've seen him ride by on his cuddy—a black donkey—and a long hat, on a Sunday morning, going towards Newcastle, when we first came here about fifty-eight years ago." Mr. Thornton agreed that he would be making for a public-house, " but it would be pure for the sport, not drink with him," and he described how he, as a boy, had seen Johnnie Anderson, who laboured for the masons, with his shovel in his hand,—they weren't very busy, bending over his shovel, and sparring the cocks,[3] or walking along talking to himself, and always about cocks, always about cocks."— Mr. James Thornton.

Mrs. Austen, cook, Cambo, who came from Cumberland, says that on her wedding day, in 1882, they saw a lot of men with game cocks going up to the fells, but the police got them.

---

[1] " Knowe . . . a bare rounded hillock."—Brocket.
[2] There are at least two rings, and they are claimed both by the fairies and the cocks.
[3] Pretending to—Mr. Thornton showed the crouched position—elbows out.

PART II

BELIEFS

CHAPTER V

GOOD AND BAD LUCK

It must be confessed that the Cambo Women's Institute have not treated this subject in a very serious spirit. The meeting, at which we discussed it, was one of the merriest we have had, and the same may be said of our older " contributors." We love and respect the remnants of our old superstitions, just as we like to keep up our old customs, but we mix our love and our respect with laughter.

Probably, each one of us has one or two pet superstitions, the Editor started with twenty-four, and dare not count again now! She must admit that she feels thoroughly uncomfortable, unless she throws salt over her left shoulder three times after spilling it, but she knows " it's just foolishness," and that is what the oldest people tell us their parents have told them, about old superstitions and fears. Miss Hilda Hedley laughs as she tells of the great heavy horseshoe she carried home, but we should most of us do the same if we were lucky enough to find one,—especially in war time. It's in our bones.

In spite of the gaiety, however, the Institute were determined only to put down what is real Cambo, and countless sayings common in other places were rejected, when mentioned by newcomers,—" not at Cambo," " No," " Not known here," or met with a dead silence or a flat contradiction.

It was difficult, in the quick talk, to be sure who gave each " belief "; and, therefore, some of our older residents have kindly gone through the list, and given their names and authority when needed, and when they agreed, that the saying was one they knew.

Customs and luck are closely connected.   One of the most universally known sayings about luck is the one, already mentioned, in connection with a universal custom :—[1]

" If a fair man or a woman come in first, they say it spoils the luck of the year."—Mrs. Forster, the Glebe Farm, White Hill.

Handsel Monday is not known at Cambo, but " at any time in the year hawkers, selling things at the door, ask you to give them a handsel.   The first buyer in the day is supposed to be lucky."—Mrs. Handyside.

" And I've seen them spit on it for luck."—Miss Shipley.

Taking Down and Burning Evergreens.

Mrs. Robert Hepple says " you must take the holly down before the 12th of January, or leave it up till Easter, but I don't know why."

Mrs. Thomas Hepple, her mother-in-law, says she had never heard this till Mrs. Robert Hepple came; she used to leave it up till Easter.

Mrs. Robert Hepple thinks you shouldn't burn the evergreens, she takes them down the wood.

Mrs. Thomas Hepple doesn't mind burning them.

" Have you ever heard it is unlucky to burn evergreens? I've always done it, but Mrs. ——[2] told me not to."—Mrs. Hedley.

This is an instance of how some customs vary, even between families who have lived here for generations.   The Murrays (Mrs. Robert Hepple's family), the Hepples, and the Pearsons (Mrs. Hedley's family) have all been here for at least a hundred years.

Luck at Christmas Time,—stirring the plum pudding, and eating mince pies, has already been mentioned.[3]

[1] Chapter I, p. 13.
[2] A resident who came from a distance, and has left again.
[3] Chapter I, p. 22.

The Baby Customs are full of luck.[1]

Wedding Customs can hardly be separated from luck.

" Green is unlucky to be married in, but a bonny lot are."
—Mrs. Thomas Hepple.

> " To be married in green
> Sorrow'll soon be seen."—Mrs. Hedley.

Mrs. Charles Trevelyan reminded us of this.

Lucky Days.

> " Monday's bairn is fair of face,
> Tuesday's bairn is full o' grace,
> Wensday's bairn is loving and giving,
> Thursday's bairn works hard for her living,
> Friday's bairn is fu' o' woe,
> Saturday's bairn has far to go,
> But the bairn that is born on the Sabbath day
> Is blythe and bonny and good and gay."
>
> —Mrs. Robert Hepple.

This may be the Scotch version, as her family (Murrays) came from over the border originally. Mrs. Keith gave a different version in Chapter III, p. 33.

Friday.

To begin anything on a Friday is unlucky; " either soon done, or never finished."—Miss Brown, of Newbiggin.

This feeling seems to be pretty strong; for instance, in connection with farming; it is considered by some people " unlucky " to begin haymaking on a Friday. There is no doubt that this is deeply rooted in the past. And there is a good deal to be said for it, as well as for many other things, which are backed up by " luck," or forbidden by " ill luck."

" A housemaid, where I was, said it wasn't lucky to *turn the mattress on a Friday,* or on a Sunday."—Mrs. Forster.

Mrs. Hedley has heard it too.

" *Sun ways round* " is right at Cambo. One of our newer residents expressed it for us at the Institute Meeting, by saying,

[1] Chapter III, pp. 33-35.

" You uncork a bottle, deal cards, or paper a wall the way of the sun."—Mrs. Gilbert Telfer, wife of chauffeur-gardener, Cambo.

And one of our oldest residents, Mrs. Thomas Hepple, confirms it, though without going into details.

The Number Thirteen.

" Some people think it is unlucky to sit down thirteen to table." [1]—Mrs. Hedley.

" Anyhow, they don't mind thirteen cards at whist! "—Somebody else at Institute Meeting.

The Last Piece of Cake.

The person to whom the last piece of cake, on a dish, is offered, and by whom it is accepted, is supposed to get " a handsome man, or £10,000 a year."—Miss Gow.

We used to be told " if you put your *boots on the table* you'll have a disappointment."—Mrs. Keith.

" I've been told that passing on the stairs is unlucky, *one* should stand."—Miss Barbara Blain,[2] housemaid, Cambo.

To cross hands, when shaking hands, *means a wedding* for one of the two, " that is if they're not married."

This was emphatically given at an Institute Meeting, in contradiction of the suggestion of a newcomer that to cross hands was unlucky.

It is unlucky to cross knives, it was mentioned at an Institute Meeting.

Mrs. Hedley explained,—if anybody comes in, and sees two knives crossed on the table it has to be put right at once, or " there'll be a row presently."

It is unlucky to give a knife, or anything that cuts as a present; to make things all right the recipient gives a halfpenny or a penny, or some other little gift in exchange. —Institute Meeting, confirmed by Mrs. Hedley.

" *It's unlucky to spill salt*, if you do, you throw some over your left shoulder, three times with right hand."—Miss Brown, at Institute Meeting. Mrs. and the Misses Hedley.

[1] The Editor's impression is that Cambo doesn't think about the number thirteen.
[2] Now Mrs. Stevenson.

" *Some people won't have a picture hanging over the door*, they say it's unlucky."—Mrs. Hedley.

" It is *unlucky if a picture falls down*."—A member at Institute Meeting.

" You *mustn't go under a ladder*."—Miss Catherine Hedley.

" It is *unlucky to break a mirror*."—Mentioned at Institute Meeting. Confirmed by Mrs. Hedley.

" It is *unlucky to pick up one's umbrella oneself*."— Miss Brown at Institute Meeting. (This is not known to us all.)

> " *See a pin and pick it up,*
>   All the day you'll have good luck,
>   See a pin and let it lie,
>   You'll need a pin before you die."

—Mentioned at Institute Meeting. Confirmed by Mrs. Hedley.

" *White heather is lucky*."—Mrs. Hedley. It is lucky to find it.

Horseshoes are supposed to *bring luck*, " but they don't always," somebody said.

" They say you ought to hang them the round way down, or else the luck will fall out. We don't trouble about hanging them the right way, but it's lucky to find one."—Miss Hilda Hedley.

" And Hilda carried a large one—one off a draught horse—a long way home, when she was doing the post round during the war! You mustn't pass one."—Mrs Hedley.

A Threesome Nut.

Miss J. D. Carr, Cambo, has a very old one, with the following description of it, in the handwriting of our grandfather, R. Carr-Ellison of Hedgeley, Northumberland. " *A threesome nut*, or triplet nut worn for good luck through many years by an old lady in her pocket. I think it was old Mrs. Hudson (Elizabeth Ellison, 1729-1815, married Henry Hudson of Whitley Hall) of Whitley.

See Ellison pedigree in Surtees' ' History of County of Durham.' She was an aunt of Miss Hannah (1769-1839)

Ellison, who long lived with her, and who was my mother's dearest friend and distant kinswoman (third cousin once removed).—(Signed) R. Carr-Ellison."

[Whitley Hall, though in Northumberland, is far outside our district.]

" I've heard of people carrying a *lucky bone* in their pockets."—Mrs. Robert Hepple.

The merry-thought is the lucky bone, so the Editor was always told as a child at Rock; we used to pull the chicken's merry-thought, and the one that got the longest bit could wish a wish; or as Mrs. Hedley puts it—the goose's, duck's, or chicken's merry-thought is pulled, and the one that gets the longest bit is the lucky one.

On the *first day of the month*, the one who can say " rabbits " first can wish a wish.—Mrs. Keith.

The Cuckoo.

" And there was I on the hard road, and not a penny in my pocket! "—Miss Hilda Hedley, repeated by her mother and sister.

" If you are standing on a hard road, when you hear the cuckoo first, it'll be a hard year for you. It's better to be on grass, and you should turn your money in your pocket."—Miss Catherine Hedley.

This has been mentioned by several people.

" When you see the *first moon* of the year, *you have to bow three times*, and wish a wish each time."—Miss H. Hedley; Mrs. Charles Trevelyan.

The above seems better known to the young people, than to the older ones. Mrs. Thomas Hepple, for instance, does not know it.

" You mustn't look at it through glass."—Mrs. Robert Hepple.

" You should *look through a new silk handkerchief at the first new moon in the year*, and as many moons as you saw would be years before you'd be married; or turn your back to the window and look at it in the looking-glass, and count the same as with the silk handkerchief."—Mrs. Hedley.

Mrs. Thomas Hepple has also referred to looking at the first moon of the year through " a silk handkerchief that has never been washed."

It is unlucky to see the new moon through glass for the first time; you should curtsy to it three times, the first time you see it, wherever you are, and turn your money in your pocket.—This was said at Institute Meeting.

If the palm of the hand is itchy, " rub it on wood, and it'll come good."—Mentioned at Institute Meeting.

" If the hand's itchy it means you'll get some money."—Miss Catherine Hedley and Mrs. Hedley.

We " tap wood," for instance, " after saying I've never had a fall from my bicycle."—Miss Catherine Hedley.

(Some of us do this instinctively almost before the sentence is out of our mouths.)

" If they don't get *a new suit at Easter*," began one of our men visitors.

" Hush," said a shocked member of the Women's Institute; —but we all know about " *the crows!* "

" *You mustn't disturb swallows;* they are lucky if they come to build their nests and have their young. Mrs. ——[1] was much afraid lest anybody should disturb them, when they came to nest by her house."—Mrs. Hedley.

Mrs. Thomas Hepple agrees that swallows should not be disturbed.

" *It's very bad when the bees die*, and they all died before the war," so one member said at an Institute Meeting. Somebody else said sceptically—" Isle of Wight disease."

Mrs. Hedley said they had lost a hive from Isle of Wight disease. " She got it up at the moors where the pitmen send their bees; suddenly they found she was dead," but no ill result followed; nobody died except the hive of bees.

> " *A swarm of bees in May*
> Is worth a cartload of hay,
> A swarm of bees in June
> Isn't worth half a croon."
>
> —Miss Bella Wilson.

---

[1] Naming somebody who came to live here for a time.

The following North Tyne version is given by Mr. Edward Keith :—

" A swarm of bees in May is worth a load of hay,
    A swarm of bees in June is worth a silver spoon,
    But a swarm of bees in July is not worth a fly."

" *May kittens* should be drowned, they are unlucky."—Miss Murray, at Institute Meeting.

" *A piebald horse is lucky*."—This was said, emphatically, at the Institute Meeting.

Mrs. George Carr-Ellison, Rothley Lodge (who comes from farther north in Northumberland), says, " so is a grey."

Miss Catherine Hedley adds, " you spit on your shoe."

" *A black cat's lucky*."[1]—Also stated with emphasis at the Institute Meeting.

" Having a fly[2] over Christmas is lucky; after Christmas you can kill it."—Miss Catherine Hedley.

Magpies.

" It is *lucky* if magpies settle down in a place."—Stated emphatically at Institute Meeting.

" One's joy,
    Two's grief,
    Three's a wedding,
    Four's death,
    Five's heaven,
    Six is hell,
    Seven's the deil's ain sel! "

—Mr. John Henderson, at an Institute Meeting.

[1] A black cat served through the war from 1914 onwards with the Northumberland Yeomanry, and is still alive at Meldon a few miles away.
[2] In the house.

" One's for sorrow,
  Two's for mirth,
  Three's a wedding,
  Four's a birth,
  Five is heaven,
  Six is hell,
  Seven's the devil's ain sel ! "

—Mrs. George Carr-Ellison.

" One's   for   sorrow,
  Two's for joy,
  Three for a girl,
  Four for a boy."

—Captain Carr-Ellison, Solicitor, Rothley Lodge, also one of an old Northumbrian family from farther north.

The ears tingling means somebody is talking about you.

" Right your Mother,
  Left your lover."

—Miss Emily Charlton.

CHAPTER VI

The Warlock at Cambo.

" My father and grandfather had this shop before me, and before them it was kept by a warlock,[1] and people daursn't owe him anything! There was a woman lived where our kitchen is now, and she kept a cow, and when she churned she used to lock the door for fear the warlock cast an evil eye on the milk and turned it sour. His shop was upstairs, that's his window that's walled up.[2] No, he never did anybody any harm. He lived to be a very old man."—Mr. George Handyside.

The old pele tower in which the shop is, was put in order for his grandparents in 1818, the date is above the window. The old warlock was alive in 1814, Mr. Handyside said.

Mrs. Thomas Hepple knew an old woman who lived where Mr. Handyside's kitchen is, she was a great friend of her mother's, and her name was Mary Wardle. On hearing about the warlock, Mrs. Hepple said, " I've heard something like that,—my mother was servant to a woman, and, when she was churning, there was something rattling about in the churn; it was a bit of rowan tree wood, to keep the cream from being turned sour by the fairies! "

Mrs. Hepple cannot say where this happened; she remembers that her mother was servant at Newbiggin, and housekeeper in Cambo.

" *Superstitions.*

In *passing a witch's house* it was considered a safeguard

---

[1] A man witch.
[2] A little square one.

to carry a sprig of *mountain ash* in your pocket (better known as *witchwood*), also when meeting the suspected person to *turn in the thumbs*.

On marriage the Bride was usually presented with a slip of *rosemary* out of the home garden, if it grew in its new home the lady was supposed to hold her own, if it died the bridegroom would be the ruler of the household.

It was also deemed very lucky to come across a *four-leaved clover*."—Written by Mrs. Keith.

The Fairies of Rothley Mill.

Two or three stories of the fairies of Rothley Mill are told in Hodgson, II. 1, p. 305 note, and other books.[1]

One of these has been told to the Editor again and again, by men and women of all ages, and is so characteristic of the wooded banks of the Hart, and still so much a part of the life of the neighbourhood that it must be included here.

" My grandfather,[2] who brought me up, used to tell me about the elves at Elf Hills. He used to tell me the story of the fairies at Rothley Mill; they made use of the mill at night, and cooked their food there. *One day the old miller threw a sod down the chimney*, and it fell into their porridge pot, and scattered the porridge all about, and they said, ' What's that? Brunt and scadded! Brunt and scadded! ' And they all rushed out and after him, and caught him at the stile to Rothley, and laid a hand on him, and he was lame ever after, and that was old Hodge the Miller!

My grandfather was very good at stories. I had Santa Claus long before anybody else had him here. On Christmas Eve he would say, ' It is time to go to bed,' and as I opened the door, ' Take care Cold Nose doesn't touch you,' and I would *start* back, almost feeling the cold nose on my hair. Some relations from America told my grandparents about Santa Claus or S. Nicholas, they even sent presents for my first stocking."—Mrs. Keith.

Mr. George Handyside's mother, who was brought up at Rothley Village, within half a mile of the Mill, used to tell him the same story, and he also tells it, laying stress on the

---

[1] Tomlinson's " Guide to Northumberland," pp. 258 and 259.
[2] Mr. Henry Codling, the joiner, who died in 1900, aged eighty.

way " *the fairies made overfree with the corn and meal*, and the miller could not have it, and set a watch."

Mr. John Henderson, who has lived sixty years in Cambo and Scots Gap, since he was a small boy, adds the detail that " the fairies used to cool their porridge in the holes in the rocks at Rothley. You'll know the round holes in the rocks, but there aren't so many now. They've put a ford there." [1] And the miller " went doubled up ever after."

" They danced at Rothley Mill too," somebody said.

Miss Arkle, Scots Gap, secretary of the Cambo District Nursing Association and formerly Sister at Newcastle Infirmary, is the daughter of Mr. Arkle who was born at Cambo; she represents a younger generation herself : —

" We used to play by the Mill as children, and think what a likely place it was for the fairies."

" And did you ever see them? "

" I dare say we thought we did! "

According to her the old miller was a hunchback ever after.

Mr. James Wilkinson of Hartington also tells the tale as it has been told to him, and mentions that the *fairies* were said to have made " *the troughs*[2] *in the rock with the miller's little picks*." He explains that " mill stones were very rough, and needed to be dressed regularly, perhaps once or twice a year," and for this purpose small picks were used, and that Mr. Moffitt, Kirkwhelpington, would know all about it.

Mr. James Moffitt, grocer and flour merchant, Kirkwhelpington, says that he has used the miller's picks himself; the handle is only about one foot long, and the pick, which goes through the handle, is only one foot long; the millstones had grooves in them, and when they got worn they had to be dressed again. He gave us one of these little old picks for exhibition at our " Treasure Evening."

Another old resident tells of " the fairy pools," another that " the fairies used to bathe there." Somebody else speaks of wicked fairies who used to come down chimneys and steal babies, and says that in the time of the old, old mill, it was not considered a safe place for babies (the *new* mill was

[1] A paved ford.
[2] Some of the holes referred to are round, some are a rough square or oblong.

burnt down in 1879 or 1880); in fact it is said to have been the headquarters of the fairies in Northumberland.

We hear rumours of " witches " at Rothley Mill; the same tale is told of them and the miller, as is told of the fairies and the miller.

Were the " witches " the wicked fairies possibly?

" My husband used to point out *the elves' track* from Elf Hills to Rothley Mill to us, it is in the field where the water is " [the wells which now supply Cambo].—Mrs. Thomas Hepple.

It was William Hepple, farmer, of Rugley Walls, " near ninety years old," who told the story of the fairies at Rothley Mill to Hodgson for his History, published in 1827.[1] The Hepples have lived a hundred and seven years at Rugley Walls, and before that at Kirk Hill.

Hodgson does not seem to have been told about the elves' track. It is still visible, running from west to east, and, as Mr. Robert Hepple explained at an Institute Meeting, is quite distinct from " the Church track."

" I think there's only the one story about Elf Hills, that *elves* danced round in a circle, and made a *ring*, and it's there yet."—Edith Henderson, of school age, Scots Gap.

Two or three other people, including Mrs. Hedley of Elf Hills, have mentioned, or pointed out, " the ring on the knowe yonder."

---

[1] Hodgson, II. 1, p. 309. It is said that when the fairies were driven away from Rothley Mill they went to Dancing Hall, near Lorbottle, in North Northumberland.

CHAPTER VII

DIVINATION, TELLING FORTUNES, AND BOGGLES

" There was *Black Jack* in Newcastle, a fortune teller, and he *could* tell fortunes. A Whalton carrier lost a forkin[1] of butter. Somebody said, ' Ye'd better see what Black Jack has to say about it.' [The answer was given before he had time to ask his question.] ' A ken weel what ye've come aboot, gang to the public-hoose at the corner, and ye'll find yer forkin, but there's nae butter in it '; and there was the forkin, but no butter."—Mr. Isaac Perceval and his housekeeper, Miss Robson.

" My mother's mother used to wash for sea captains; ain day a' the shirts were gane. My mother's father said, ' Ask Black Jack '; she went til' him, and as she came in he said, ' Ye'll find the shirts on the kitchen table when ye gang hame. It was your guid neighbour that took them.' And there they were. That will be seventy years since."—Miss Robson.

" No, he wasn't a black man.[2]

There was a woman that couldn't get her butter to come; she churned, and she churned, and she churned, and it *wouldn't* come. Black Jack told her to take a *sheep's heart,* and hang it up in the chimney, and *stick pins into it,* and her that had wished her would appear. If you have been wished by anyone, take a sheep's heart, and hang it over the fire, and stick pins in it.

Three young men were going to Newcastle to the market and as they went over the fells, one said to the other, ' We'll hae a bit o' fun wi' Black Jack afore the market begins.'

---

[1] Forkin or firkin is a little butter barrel.
[2] The following stories explain the meaning of his name.

When they got to Black Jack he gave them three chairs close in front o' the fire, and it burnt hotter, and hotter, and hotter, and they *couldn't* move their chairs back.

At last he let them go. ' A heard what ye were saying coming ower the fells, " We'll hae a bit o' fun wi' Black Jack," and A've had a bit o' fun wi' *ye!* ' "—Mr. Isaac Perceval.

Telling Fortunes.

Probably all of us, as children, have told our fortunes with " the leaf of an ash," or daisy petals, or fruit stones. The following versions were given at an Institute Meeting:—

> " Tinker, tailor,
>   Soldier, sailor,
>   Rich man, poor man,
>   Beggarman, thief."

" Coach, carriage, wheelbarrow, cart."

" Big house, little house, pigsty, barn."

" This year, next year, sometime, never."

The First Lamb you see in the year—the way the lamb's facing—that way you'll travel.[1] Mrs. Keith says, " We, as children, used to take this as meaning—that way we'd go for our holidays, we were settled here, and never thought of moving. The shepherds and those that moved often, would understand it as meaning—that they would go to live north or south."

" The first lamb of the season you see, the way the lamb's looking, that way you're going to live; it may be north, or it may be south, it may be east, or it may be west. And it comes true often. When we were in service, often we would say, we would go out and see the lambs, often we laughed about it. When we were at Otterburn Hall, we weren't any of us thinking of leaving, and four of us went out to see the lambs, and there wasn't two of us saw a lamb facing the

---

[1] Can this be an old saying of the days of the border raiders? See Chapter XXII, p. 152,—of the Scots burning Great Bavington—" in the troublesome times as they travelled they burned."

same way, and we all left together, and went different directions, the way they were facing."—Miss Robson.

Divination by Dream, and Hidden Treasure.

" On a Sunday morning, Bulmer, or Bolam,[1] went to axe the shoemaker, Rogerson, for to go with him, that he'd dreamed about some money, and he had a spade and a poke[2] with him; and the shoemaker wouldn't have anything to do with it, thought he'd gone out of his heid. Bulmer said he'd dreamed several times that he put down three sticks and digged at the middle one, and found a brown jug. And sure enough when he dug at the middle stick he found a brown jug, and he broke the pot in lifting it, and it was full of money, and he gave part away to people round, the rest was claimed by the revenue, by the lord of the Manor. That was on Throp Hill farm,[3] when I was seven years old, that is seventy-one years ago, and I've seen a bit of the jug. Fenwick had a bit of the jug. I think it was old money, but I was too young to know what kind."—Dictated by Mr. Isaac Perceval.

It should be mentioned that hidden treasure plays a larger part in our lives than is the case in most places. Many of the stories of " Meg o' Meldon," and of Hartington Hall, refer to the discoveries of her hoards, but are so well given in books that we have not gone into them;[4] and there are records of many other findings of treasure, hidden during the troubled times, for instance, the Roman vessels of silver in Silver Lane, on the way to Capheaton, scarcely three miles from here in 1747;[5] and a great store of coins in the Fenwick Tower, near Stamfordham to the south in 1775;[6] the Fenwicks were at Wallington in the sixteenth and seventeenth centuries.

Even in the nineteenth and twentieth centuries, when a family, or an individual, come into possession of unaccount-

---

[1] There was uncertainty as to the exact name.

[2] " A poke, a bag, a sack."—Brocket.

[3] Near Mitford.

[4] See Tomlinson's " Guide to Northumberland, pp. 255 and 259; Hodgson, " History of Northumberland," Vol. II, Part II, pp. 11 and 12; " In the Troublesome Times," Chapter XXI, p. 148.

[5] Tomlinson, p. 238; Hodgson, II, I, p. 228 note; British Museum, " Guide to Antiquities of Roman Britain," pp. 90-93, with illustrations.

[6] Tomlinson, p. 84.

able wealth, stories are told of how they are believed to have found it, or it is said " there must be a gold mine somewhere."

Boggles[1]

The Editor knows particulars of, and authorities for, several places where there were supposed to be boggles, but it seems scarcely worth while to risk re-awakening the superstitious fears which were felt by the children and young people of a generation ago, by enumerating these, when there is no special antiquarian or historical interest attached. Her impression is, that wherever human remains were found, boggles were feared, for a few years after. How many grim discoveries there were, in the first centuries of peace, after the long years of raids, and battles, and lawlessness! But she must admit that Mr. George Charlton does not agree with her theory, and has quite a different explanation:—

" There were boggles every road when I was a laddie." [2] —Mr. George Charlton.

But he says there were no real boggles. He thinks a man and a sheet were often the cause of the boggle! The last boggle he heard of, at Haydon Bridge, was proved to be a man wrapped in a sheet, just frightening people, and Miss J. D. Carr remembers that in North Northumberland, near Stamford, a boggle quickly disappeared, after the late Earl Grey had made it known that he was going to shoot it.

The boggles, in any case, seem to have been far more feared than seen. None of our authorities own to having seen one.

With boggles, as with sayings about luck, it seems likely that they were made use of in support of parental authority. " Mind you come home quick from school to-night, remember you've got to come past —— " and I used to *run*, for it was a spot where a skull, or a body had been found lightly buried.

In another place outside our district there was said to have been a battle, and there was a mound where the children were afraid to play.

There were once two brothers and a sister. The brothers went out to meet the Scots, leaving their sister, hidden in a

---

[1] " A boggle . . . a spectre or ghost."—Brocket.
[2] See Chapter XXIV, pp. 168 and 170.

secret hiding-place—the secret of which was known to no one else—in the wall of a room of their stronghold. They fought, and both brothers were killed; the sister could never be found; only her ghost has been seen in the room.

A lady of high degree had greatly loved a beautiful home. When she had to leave it, she gave directions that, after her death, the funeral procession should be brought past the house, where she had spent her happiest years. Her wishes were carried out, but there was a thick mist, and at a desolate spot, approaching the old home, the driver lost his way, and went to find out where he was. On his return the coffin was empty.

So the stories go.

CHAPTER VIII

SIMPLES AND OTHER CURES

" *Chickweed*, out of the garden, is very good for a sore back; you drink it.

A good lotion can be made from *elderberries* for eczema. They are good for colds too.

A flower called *shepherd's crook*,[1] a little white flower," is made into a drink for diarrhœa. [An instance of a cure was given.]

" One day a mugger[2] woman came here, and she said, ' You don't know the use of that flower, or you would have it all gathered; it's good for a sore back.' It was a pink flower."—Mrs. Craig, wife of shoemaker, Close House.

" We use *merse*, it's good for all sorts of things, even for cancer," and Mrs. Hall described how they had used it for such a case, " to bathe the wound, and it soothed it, and prevented the smell."—Mrs. Hall, wife of farmer, Hartington Hall.

Her daughter said the same, but called it " *marsh mallow*."

" We mask[3] *centaury*, and it's good for the stomach. It doesn't grow in these parts, but grew where we came from.[4] Also *bettany*.

Violet leaves make a good poultice for anything."—Miss Hall.

" There's a flat leaf, I think it's *docken*, which is good for healing cuts, you lay it on the cut."—Miss Bella Wilson (postwoman during the war.)

---

[1] Shepherd's crook seems to be the same as shepherd's purse—*bursa pastoris*.
[2] Hawker.
[3] Infuse.
[4] Farther east.

" I've had my throat gargled with *sage*. Mother used to get a little sup vinegar, perhaps a cupful, and a good handful of sage leaves, and she put it in a pan and boiled it, and then I had to gargle with it, and it took the rawness off. I used to have desperate bad throats."—Dictated by Mrs. Hedley.

Mrs. Shade also says, " We use sage to gargle with, for a sore throat; water is poured on it, and it is masked."

Camomile Tea.

" If your stomach was out of order, or you had a headache. Mr. Handyside's mother sold the flowers. Mother would send us for perhaps an ounce of *camomile* flowers, and she put them in a jug, and filled the jug up with boiling water, let it stand till it cooled, and then Mother made us drink a saucerful, and oh, dear, it was bitter! Some people had it in the garden. There was an old man called Hugh Weddell who had his camomile bed,[1] and they kept them, and dried them on a sunny day, and turned them over. I've never seen them since I was a girl."—Dictated by Mrs. Hedley.

Horehound was used " for the stomach too, made in exactly the same way as camomile tea, but it had stalks, you broke it up and put it in the jug." It was even nastier than camomile tea!

Bogbean was another, but I never tasted it, and I forget what it was for.—Mrs. Hedley.

Foxgloves. Mr. Anderson of the Shiel told Mrs. Hedley that his father used to make ointment from them. His father was born at Milkhope on Cheviot.

Wells.

" Stinky " is a well with *iron* water near Cambo village. " The doctors used to order it for people who weren't well." —Mrs. Thomas Hepple.

It is considered good for anæmic persons, or for those with a tendency to goitre; there is lime in the water which is laid on to Cambo now, so water is still sometimes fetched from " Stinky," a field away. There are several wells near

---

[1] At Cambo. The particular garden was described.

together—Jimmy's Well (marked on Ordnance Survey), and, farther on along " the Bridle Path," Hepple's, Stinky and another.

Mrs. Thomas Hepple, as a girl, living in Cambo, used to fetch water from one of these wells, carrying it up the bank, on her head, on a weeze, or roll made out of an old stocking. " What a fechting I got when my new tin can fell down and got damaged! "

" Stinky " is the middle one with red water; the water for the village used to be fetched from it, and the plantation gets the name of Stinky from it."—Mr. John Robinson, who has the field in which Stinky is.

" There is a *Sulphur* well at Kirkwhelpington."—A member at Institute Meeting.

" People come to Kirkwhelpington in summer for the sulphur well, but it has never become known."—Mr. James Wilkinson.

Bonesetters.

There have been, and still are in Northumberland, men, who without passing through medical schools have acquired skill in putting in joints that are out, and putting on " leaders " that are off. Especially in old days, endless tales were told of cases where the bonesetters succeeded in putting right what doctors had failed to do.

The most famous of these bonesetters was the late Isaac Milburn, and some of the others were his pupils. Several tales about him will be told in the next part—Chapter XIV, pp. 111-113.

CHAPTER IX

WEATHER SIGNS

Signs of Rain.

The short unfinished bit of a rainbow, near the horizon, is " *the weather gall*," [1] you see it in haytime, when there's rain about.—Mrs. Thomas Hepple.

It is also spoken of as " a weather ga'." We don't like it, it is a sign of change.

" It is generally seen in the morning, it must be the position of the sun; it is broader than a rainbow, and not so bright. It very often is followed by bad weather."—Mr. James Thornton.

" I've heard them say that the rainbow, the bit of the rainbow, is a weather ga'."

" When the red is along the sea coast, and goes back on to the sea, we're going to have a fine day; but if it comes over on to the land, we're going to have wet; and I think it's true. I've an aunt who'll tell you pretty well how many hours till it'll rain. I've seen it rain by twelve o'clock."—Dictated by Mrs. Robert Hepple.

" *Red sky in the morning* is the shepherd's warning.
Red sky at night is the shepherd's *delight*."

—Miss Tissie Graham, shopkeeper, Scots Gap, and Mrs. Oliver, Cambo.

Mrs. Oliver prefers the following:—

> " *Rainbow in the morning*,
> Shepherd's warning;
> Rainbow at night,
> Shepherd's delight."

[1] See " Weather ga' " in Brocket, and " Weather-gaw " in Heslop.

This was also given to us by the late Rev. C. A. Fitch, Vicar at Cambo for thirty-three years, and by Miss Catherine Hedley.

" *The Ark* "—" white streaks right across the sky, sometimes they lie one way, sometimes the other, the shape of the Ark. If the wind is blowing into it, it means good weather; if the wind is blowing against it, it upsets it, and it will rain in twenty-four hours."—Miss and Mrs. Oliver, Cambo, formerly of the Post Office.

" *Noah's Ark*,—the form of a boat bottom in the sky, broad in the middle, narrow at each end; I can hardly remember, but I think north-east and south-west is a good way, and that Tynemouth to Howick Hole is a bad one."—Mrs. Thomas Hepple.

" It looks like rain, I always think a *streaky sky* looks like rain; a *mackerel sky* it's sure to rain after."—Mrs. Oliver.

" If *Simonside* "[1] has her nightcap on in the morning, it's sure to rain.—Mrs. and Miss Oliver. Mrs. Hedley heartily confirms this as a Cambo saying.

" If *Angerton lake*[2] is very shiny and clear in the morning, it's sure to rain."—Mrs. Oliver.

" Or the sea," [2] add Mrs. Hedley and her daughters.

" When I was going out to work in the morning, if *Cambo Church Tower* was clear, I knew it would be a fine day; if it were thick in a cloud, I knew we'd have bad weather." —Mr. Isaac Perceval, formerly keeper at Angerton, east of Cambo.

" If the *Cock crows* when he goes to bed,
He's sure to wake with a watery head."

—Miss Hilda Hedley, Miss Catherine Hedley and Mrs. Keith.

" It's a bad sign if he crows when he gets on his perch." —Mrs. Hedley.

" *Crickets make a big noise* when there's going to be rain." —Mrs. Hedley.

---

[1] Simonside is a conspicuous upstanding hill to the north of Cambo perhaps eight or ten miles away.

[2] Angerton Lake is a couple of miles east of Cambo; the sea is a long way off, and can only be seen to the south-east on clear days; so the mere fact of seeing the sea, in the morning, is a warning.

" It's considered a sign of rain *when the cat lies with its
back to the fire,* or when washing puts its paw over its ear."
—Miss Emily Charlton.

" When the cat *sits up* with its back to the fire," is Mrs.
Hedley's version; whilst Miss Jessie Carr, Cambo, who comes
from another part of Northumberland, says it is a fact that
when the cat lies on its head, there will be rain !

" *When the swallows are flying low,* it is a sign of rain."
—Mrs. Keith and Mrs. Hedley.

Signs of Fine Weather.

" *Rain before seven,*
Fine before eleven."

—Miss Emily Charlton.

The red sky, the rainbow, Cambo Church tower have
already been mentioned in connection with signs of rain, and
the reverse.

Signs of Wind.

" My Mother always used to say that when there's *goat's
hair* in the sky, it was a sign of wind."—Mrs. Hedley (her
mother was born at Rothley Village).

" What we call *shepherd's flock*—flying clouds—foretells a
storm."—Mrs. Austen, who was born in Cumberland.

" *Red sky in the morning* means wind."—Mrs. Graham,
Wallington, who came from Cumberland twenty years ago,
and Mrs. Hedley.

Other Signs of a Storm.

" *When the cattle and sheep are jumping and playing,* it's
a sign of bad weather."—Mrs. Oliver.

" *When the cat's frisky,* in winter, there's a storm coming."
—Miss Hilda Hedley.

" When she goes round like a top, as our cat does, when
she has a gale in her tail," as Mrs. Oliver puts it.

" *A brough,*" or ring *round the moon,* is a sign of bad
weather.

" A far off brough means a near at hand storm; a near

brough means a far off storm."—Mr. Gilbert Telfer, confirmed by Mr. George Charlton.

" A wide brough " is the way Mrs. Oliver puts it.

Some Signs of Snow.

" *We smell it.*"—Miss McCracken, Mrs. Rutherford.

" *Snowpacks.*" Heavy white clouds, " but when you see them it's ready to fall."—Mr. John Henderson.

" *The tits*, and other small birds, *go in flocks* before a snowstorm."—Mrs. Keith.

Signs of a Thaw.

" *It's never a right thaw when the wind's in the east.*" —Miss Hilda Hedley.

" *The wind* ought *to go round to* the *west by* the *south*; it's bad if the wind backs."

" It should go *sunways round.*"—Mrs. Oliver.

In speaking of a hard frost, most of us say, " The frost has never given to-day," but Mrs. Oliver has a pretty saying, " *The frost has never shed a tear to-day.*"—Quoted by Mrs. Gilbert Telfer.

" *There's always rain after three white frosts.*"—Mr. George Charlton.

In another part of Northumberland, near the sea, we found this very true. The three white frosts were a real warning to complete an outside job before the weather broke.—Miss R. E. Bosanquet.

The Moon and Stars were more believed in as weather signs by a former generation than they are to-day in Cambo.

" *Shooting stars* are reckoned a sign of rain by some people, but I don't think there's much in it."

" *If the moon is lying on her back* she is a bad one; and if she's *got the old one in her arms* it's bad. *If* she's *too soon seen*, it's a bad sign."—Mrs. Oliver gives these sayings; Mrs. Hedley and Miss Hilda Hedley confirm them.

Mrs. Oliver quotes the old saying:—

" *A Saturday's change* on a Sunday's prime,
    Was never a good one in any man's time."

" *The weather often changes with the moon.*"

G

Sayings About Special Days, Months, and Seasons.
> " If the wind's in the east on *Candlemas Day*
> There it will stick till the second of May."
> > —A member at Institute Meeting.

> " If Candlemas Day be fair and clear,
> The half of the winter's to come, and more,
> If Candlemas Day be dark and foul,
> The half of the winter's gone at Yule."
> > —Miss and Mrs. Oliver.

Mrs. Hedley gives the same, except that her second line runs:—

> " The half of winter is but here."

" If Candlemas Day be fair and clear,
> The hinds may put on their mittens and mourn all the year."
> > —Mrs. Oliver.

> " *February fill dyke,*
> Either black or white."
> > —Mr. Edwin Pearson, postman, Cambo.

" *If March comes in like a lion*, it will go out like a lamb."
—Miss Emily Charlton, Mrs. Oliver, Mrs. Hedley, all confirm it as a common saying.

" *When the sun crosses the line* (on the twenty-first of March), where the wind is, there it will stay for three months.
If the wind's in the east when the sun crosses the line, it will be a dry summer; if it's in the west it will be a wet summer."—Mr. John Henderson, and Mr. Robert Hepple, at an Institute Meeting.

Mr. James Thornton has no faith in this.

> " *March borrowed of April*
> Three days and they were ill,
> The first was sleet,
> The second was sna',
> And the third yin
> Was the warst amang them a'." [1]
> > —Miss Hilda Hedley; Miss Murray.

[1] We know that there is more of this, which can be read in books.

" These are what we call *the borrowing days*."—Mrs. Hedley.

> " *March winds and April sun*
> Make clothes white and maidens dun." [1]

—At Institute Meeting this was mentioned. Mrs. Oliver and Mrs. Hedley confirm it.

> " *Cast not a thread,*
> *Till May be dead.*"

—Mrs. Gilbert Telfer from Mrs. Oliver.

> " *Cast not a clout*
> *Till May be out.*"

—Mrs. Gilbert Telfer; Mrs. Pearson, Dovecot.

" Don't cast a clout," etc.—Mrs. Hedley.

> " *Oak before the ash,*
> Then there'll be a splash.
> Ash before the oak,
> Then we'll have a soak."

—Miss Emily Charlton; Mrs. Hedley.

If it is fine on *St. Swithin's* Day, it will be fine for forty days.

If it is wet on St. Swithin's, it will rain every day for forty days.

This is a common saying, and was mentioned at an Institute Meeting. Certainly we often do have a long spell of wet weather after that date, and we always notice what the weather is that day; but one of the young men of Cambo declared this year that it was " only an old superstition," and the next day did seem to be absolutely dry, breaking the spell.

Mr. James Thornton has no faith in it.

> " *A lot of haas*
> A lot of snaas."

—Miss Murray.

" Plenty of berries foretells a hard winter," but Miss Hilda Hedley noticed a year not long ago when there were lots of berries and a mild winter.[2]

The last two instances are given to show that our old

---

[1] " Dun, a yellowish brown colour."—Heslop.
[2] Since this was written we have had the open winter of 1922-23, whilst the hedges were red with haws till spring.

weather sayings are constantly quoted as showing what the weather is likely to be, but that we do not always find them right. We are interested to see whether they do, or do not come true. We take into consideration the state of the barometer, and the state of the wind at the same time. " With the wind where it is, and the barometer going down . . ."

PART III

STORIES AND MUSIC

CHAPTER X

THE LIFTING OF THE DAPPLE GREY MARE, AND THE KINE FROM
RODLEY

THIS traditional tale may now be read in Mr. Edward Keith's
novel, " The Keeper of the Rede " (published, 1929, by
Andrew Reid, Newcastle-upon-Tyne), pp. 27-30. He gave the
account of how he heard the legend in the following letter : —

WALLINGTON GARDEN HOUSE,
CAMBO,
July, 1922.

The bare outlines of this story, with the names of the
Reivers, and their place of abode, and the place names of
Rodley,[1] Greenleighton and Rothbury Forest, with a very
incorrect description of the route covered by the Redesdale
Thieves, was among other legends many times recited to me,
when a boy, by a great aunt (a Charlton) some forty-four years
ago. The old lady was then in her eighty-fifth year and was
a perfect mine of legendary lore relating to North Tyne and
Upper Redesdale. In her teens, which would be about one
hundred and twenty-four years ago, her father worked one of
the small moorland coal pits, between Bellingham and Otterburn, and his family of five daughters, regularly as their
share of the work, carried the produce on the backs of a
string of hill ponies over the Carter into Jeddert (Jedburgh).
Leading this romantic life, and brought daily into contact
with the Borderers on both sides of the Divide, naturally they
would hear all the tales (true and legendary) handed down

---

[1] The Rodley Village and Rodley Crags of this story are identical with
the Rothley Village and Rothley Crags of other parts of this book. Both
spellings were used in old maps, and both pronunciations are used to-day.

by bygone generations. The mention of the monk of New-minster and the exile of the Percy family, places the date of the story right back into the fifteenth century, but when we consider, if told to the narrator in her teens by an old Elsdonian, this would cover well over two hundred years, and it is quite reasonable to think, that, during the other two hundred and sixty odd years the story may have been handed down from generation to generation fairly accurate. As the story was told with great relish by my relative without any reference to the morality of the undertaking, it may be assumed, that the story would survive longer in this district, where the people were proud of the adventure, than among those who were cleverly outwitted. I have taken the liberty to re-write the whole story, founded on the fragments my memory recalls, for it was long before I knew there was such a place as Cambo, that these old legends of Redesdale became familiar to me."

CHAPTER XI

OUR oft told tale of *the Miller of Rothley Mill and the Fairies*
has been given, in connection with " Beliefs," in Chapter VI,
p. 83.

Mr. Edward Keith thinks " the story must go back a long
way, the Mill went back to the days of the Fenwicks." [1]

The Miller of Wallington.

There are traces of another mill, close to " the Fenwicks'
Drive," from Wallington Bridge [along the north bank of
the Wansbeck] up to Wallington.—Mr. Edward Keith.

Mrs. Keith remembers her grandfather—Mr. Henry
Codling—taking her to the site of Wallington Mill,—" the
place is still pointed out—the old grindstone half buried and
the three thorn trees inside the iron railing, which are called
' the Miller's Garden.' "

Mr. William Embleton and Mrs. Batey (his daughter) have
shown to the Editor a story, related by John Stokoe in " North
Country Lore and Legend " (1890), p. 421, that the old Miller of
Wallington—Anderson—put the present words to the still
older small pipe tune of " Shew me the way to Wallington,"
which he was in the habit of playing on the small pipes.

This story is given in greater detail with the song in
Chapter XX, but a few facts, connected with them, may be
mentioned now.

No road leads past the site of the mill now. " The
Fenwicks' Drive " turned up before the Mill to Wallington
Hall; Sir Charles Trevelyan improved it, forty years ago, for

[1] A mill existed there at least as far back as 1261. See Hodgson,
II, I, pp. 306 and 307.

Eleanora, Lady Trevelyan to use as a grass drive, but the old men told Mr. Keith that it dated back to the Fenwicks, and that the old, old road to Kirkwhelpington went the same way along the north bank of the Wansbeck, and that road can be traced past the mill and joining the present road near Greaves Dean. This old road was superseded by Sir Walter Blackett's roads; Sir Walter Blackett came to Wallington in 1728. Our local poet, Thomas Whittell, who died in 1736, in his poem on the marriage of Sir William Blackett, Bart., with the Lady Barbara Villiers in 1725, describes festivities on Shaftoe Crag—

> " The pipe's sweet air made all as gay as June,
>   The way to Wallington was still the tune."

The " Piper's Chair " is the name for one of the largest rocks on Shaftoe Crag.

According to Mackenzie's " Northumberland," Vol. II, p. 162 note, published 1825, Thomas Whittell was engaged by a miller when he came to Cambo " about the beginning of the last century," and remained with him some years.

It seems possible therefore, to the Editor, that Anderson, the piper miller of Wallington, was the employer of the boy poet, Whittle, or Whittell, and that the Sir William Blackett, who married in 1725, was the open-handed lord of Wallington, referred to in Chapter XX, pp. 127, 128. The Mill figures on a map at Wallington as late as 1777.

Anderson is a well-known name here. Even to-day there is a piper of a family of that name in our district. Mrs. Armstrong of High Hartington, daughter of the late Mr. Anderson of Rothley Shiel, can play the small pipes, or Northumbrian pipes.

With her permission, we quote from a poem, written about her as a girl:—

> " She lo'ed to play the auld pipe tunes
>   Where fern and heather vary,
>   And wha is it that hesna heerd
>   O' bonny ' Piper Mary.'
>
> Na'e wonder that men lo'e to come,
>   Frae places far and near;
>   And hear her as she softly plays,
>   The pipe tunes lo'ed sae dear."

(N.S.)

Thomas Whittell.

" Tradition says he was first seen riding into Cambo on an old ram. I have some of his work here [Wallington Winter Garden] and very good work it is too [an old sundial with date 1733]. It used to be above the door of the blacksmith's old cottage, since restored. He did all the sundials here.

It was a relation of Mrs. Keith's, a Codling, who got Whittell's Poems printed [in 1815]; he had the manuscript, and took it with him to Jamaica, and sent it back to be printed; but the ship's captain, to whom it was entrusted, was so pleased with it, that it was very difficult to recover it from him.[1]

There is some painting of Whittell's on a wardrobe at Harnham.[2] He was a queer fellow who never stayed long at one thing.

Another thing he did, which the old man used to tell me, he hollowed out one of the holes in the rock at Shaftoe,— enlarged it with a chisel, and made what is called the Devil's Punch Bowl. This was filled with whatever liquor they drank in those days, and they all sat up, and drank it, at the time when Sir William Blackett,—the one Sir George does not like—was getting married.[3] And I think the story was right, for they got the lady's name—Lady Villiers, and so she was. It was a party given by Vaughan of East Shaftoe, in honour of his landlord—Sir William Blackett. Other people say the Punch Bowl had to do with Druidical worship, and no doubt there are traces of a British Camp near.

Thomas Whittell was buried at Hartburn; Mr. Codling of Hartburn has pointed out his grave to me, just inside the Churchyard gate. There is no stone."—Mr. Edward Keith, whose wife's grandfather, Mr. Henry Codling, lived with him and Mrs. Keith, for his last years, till his death in 1900, aged eighty. Mr. Henry Codling, and his fore-elders,[4] were joiners, and worked for the Trevelyans, and before them for the Blacketts, at Wallington.

[1] Compare preface, dated 1815, to " The Poetical Works of Thomas Whittell."
[2] Described in Chapter IV, p. 62.
[3] See above, p. 104.
[4] Ancestors, relations of an older generation.

CHAPTER XII

THE JACOBITE RISINGS OF 1715 AND 1745

The 1715.

" Tradition says that *Lord Derwentwater* hid in the cave at Shaftoe Crags.—Mr. Edward Keith.

" For three weeks "—Miss L. Robson of East Shaftoe says.

" A dog from Shortflatt fed him for a fortnight, while he was concealed in the cave. There is supposed to be an underground passage from Capheaton to the cave. They've tried to find it from the cave but never could."—Miss Edith Lamb, now Mrs. Stephen Fairbairn, Scots Gap.

Shortflatt[1] is considered one of the finest keeps in Northumberland.—Miss L. Robson.

Miss Brown of Newbiggin (farmer) has a mirror, which she has always been told, was bought at Lord Derwentwater's sale by an ancestress of hers.

The 1745.

Sir Charles Trevelyan, my grandfather, used to mention that when he first came to Wallington, he used to talk to a man, who remembered the troopers riding down Cambo bank, on their way back from Culloden in 1745. Probably he was at Wallington about 1822-1825 before he went to India.

The stock of sherry found in Wallington cellars in 1878 on Sir Walter Trevelyan's death was said to have been laid in, in 1745, to regale the Duke of Cumberland's officers on their way back after that victory.—Written by Mr. Charles Trevelyan, M.P.[2]

[1] On the east side of Shaftoe.
[2] Now Sir Charles Trevelyan.

CHAPTER XIII

" At one time they got what they could, and sold it to the Chevy Chase[1]; it wasn't poaching, for it wasn't forbidden, and there would only be one gamekeeper in ten miles. Then the landowners took to preserving.

I served my time [as keeper] with John Turnbull at Meldon, he had a broken nose.

The nailers from Tyneside used to come over with their lurchers, and the farmers came out, and he had to go out too, and there was a fight, and Turnbull was hurt. It was somewhere up to the west. There was a park wall, with holes at the bottom for the hares to go through, but a dog couldn't, or only a small dog. Some of the lurchers went over, but they never came back.

They used to take sheep, and give the mutton to their dogs, that was what set the farmers so against them."—Mr. Isaac Perceval.

In the thirties there was a gang of miners, who openly infested the moors round Simonside, marching in line with guns. The gentry at length came out armed with their keepers. The two parties met on the Wallington moors and the poachers surrendered without fighting. As they were being driven along the Gibbet Road, one of the poachers, with handcuffs on, jumped off the cart, in which they were being taken to prison, and ran over the Harwood Head moor, towards Catcherside. He was recaptured.—Written by Mr. Charles Trevelyan.

Tod Hall. Sheep-stealing story.

In the most isolated part of the moorland south of Tosson

[1] The coach from Newcastle to Edinburgh via Cambo and Harwood Gate.

and Simonside, one mile south-east of Darden Lough, is the spot which is marked as Tod Knowe (at the end of Tod Craig) in the Ordnance Map. Under the lee of Tod Knowe, facing southward, is a ruin of a house (1922), marked in Wallington Estate maps of 1777 as Tod Hall. It was built subsequently to 1728 as other maps at Wallington show. It was always in the Wallington Estate. A few hundred yards from it to south-west are the still older and more ruined relics of the township of Fallow Shiel, which had fallen into ruin by 1777 according to the map. Tod Hall may possibly have been built out of these ruins.

The old gamekeeper of the Wallington Estate, Tom Thornton, used to tell a story about Tod Hall. I remember his telling it to me in sight of the place, when I was a boy. I have compared notes of my recollections with Mr. Shade, the present keeper, and the story is as follows:—

A man used to inhabit Tod Knowe (probably in first years of nineteenth century, possibly end of eighteenth), who was a sheep stealer. Some of his neighbours, not being able to obtain legal proof of his depredations, proceeded to put marked sheep into his flocks with a view to fabricating evidence against him. Death was then the penalty. He detected the sheep, drove them away, but was so much frightened that he left the countryside.[1]—Written by Mr. G. M. Trevelyan,[2] author of " British History in the Nineteenth Century," etc.

The Prize Fight at Middleton Brig.[3]

It started on the moors north of Newcastle, but they were disturbed by the constables. They fought it out at Middleton Brig, but it got dark, and the black man could see the white man, but the white man couldn't see the black man, so blackie won. He was Molyneux; Renwick was the white man.—Mr. Walter Hedley.

Mr. John Robinson says " the fight was finished at Middleton Brig; they'd been driving round from place to place with the constables after them. Hepple of Black

---

[1] Another version of this story lays more stress on the appalling harshness of the laws at that time, and suggests that possibly the farmer at Tod Knowe was not a sheep stealer, but that those who had a spite against him put the marked sheep amongst his, and the danger of being condemned to death was too great a risk for him to face.

[2] Now Regius Professor of History at Cambridge.

[3] M. A. Richardson's " Table Book," Vol. IV, p. 399, supplies the date October 31st, 1837, but not all the same details.

Heddon told me of it, he was there. He'd have been one hundred if he'd been alive now."

Mr. Edward Keith writes " My mother's version of the story was that the fight was disturbed at Middleton Brig by the Sheriff, or his officers. They coached on to the Five Lane Ends (near Colwell, on the Hexham road), and there finished the encounter, the last of its brutal kind in Northumberland. She saw Renwick at Bellingham, in or about the same year, when he was lionized by the public, a regrettable proof of a brutal age.

" *Dick Stamp* was a cockfighter, and a rabbit catcher, and many a hare he caught too; one time he put a string round the neck of a hare, and led it right through Longhirst[1] Street just to annoy Mr. Lawson. He couldn't have done it now with the present law.

There'd been some grievance between him and Mr. Lawson, and in those days they couldn't fine you unless the keeper caught you on the ground; you could carry as many rabbits and hares, and pheasants as you liked! Dick was eighty-six when he died, and I was only fourteen or fifteen. I can't remember seeing him."—Mr. Isaac Perceval.

The Muckle Cairn.

" The story goes—that they were fox-hunting on that crag; and the fox, and the horse, and the man, and the dogs—all went over the crag—we were told it as children, but we never found anything to show it was true. The Muckle Cairn is the largest rock below Rothley Castle."—Miss Murray.

Ga'en Folk.

Donkin Rig was a great harbour for going folk (ga'en folk)—gipsies and the like, and somebody, listening outside the byre, at a lunkit hole,[2] heard them discussing the division of the spoil, and a child said " My mother maun get maist,[3] she stealed maist."—Dictated by Miss McCracken, from Dr. McCracken.

---

[1] Longhirst is a village some fourteen miles east of Cambo, not itself on the moors.
[2] The slit for air at the cow's head.
[3] " Must get most."

CHAPTER XIV

TALES OF WHISKY SMUGGLING AND OF ISAAC MILBURN

" Mrs. ——'s uncle was smuggling whisky once; he had it in a keg, and they were after him; and they got hold of his reins, so he cut the mare's reins, and got away leaving the reins in their hands, and he put the mare in the pen among the calves, and went across the Hart, on to a high place, where he could watch them.   And when the excisemen came and searched the farm, the calves thought it was some-one to feed them, and they all pressed forward, and the excisemen never saw the mare!   When the excisemen were gone, out came Mrs ——'s uncle, and took the mare, and the whisky from among the calves.   It was supposed he went to the neighbourhood of Blyth with the whisky, and he sold the mare and the whisky, and went to America.   He'd been fined £45, or £50, last time, not long before, and he thought he might be transported.   It was his brother told me about it, and it would be about one hundred years ago.

They used to bring whisky over from Scotland; they would get it there for 8d. or 1od. the three gill bottle.   I mind my mother buying a bottle at the door for 18d.; it must have been smuggled for the price.   The man had a flat tin on his back that fitted his back, and a big coat on top of it.

I once found what must have been a *spirit still* in the corner of a field and burn, by a little wood they call Tommy's Island, at Meldon; there was a bit of a bog across it.   It has all been ploughed since.   I was digging out a rabbit, and it came out all sooty, and I dug deeper, and came on flues.   I made inquiries round about, and was told it must have been a still.   It was just the place for it, water and all; dripping water is needed, and there was the worm."—Mr. Isaac Perceval.   He was keeper at Meldon, as well as at Angerton.

The last fight with the smugglers was at Deanham Gate. This is quite true, I had it from Mr. Henry Codling.   The excisemen happened to be coming from Hexham, and they met the smugglers,—it was the only bit of road the smugglers had been on. There was a great fight, and the excisemen were badly hurt. They were taken to Wallington. Isaac Milburn[1] was keeper at Wallington then; he took his gun, and another man went with him, and they overtook the smugglers at Shortflatt and took them. Milburn said he'd shoot them if they didn't give in. And they were sent to Jamaica or Australia. It was in Sir John Trevelyan's time.— Mr. Edward Keith.

Isaac Milburn was keeper at Wallington; he used to practise on the broken bones of rabbits. He was called away so often for *bonesetting* that at last Sir Walter Trevelyan gave him his choice of being either a gamekeeper, or a bonesetter; so he gave up being a keeper.

Once he was sent for to a great lady near London, who had put her hip out, and all the great doctors were bet.[2] The Duke's footman met him at the station. " Are you Mr. Milburn? " " I'se *Isaac* Milburn anyway! " He was taken into the lady's room, there were three black-coated doctors there, and he turned them all out, then he set the hip, and she walked round the room.—Mr. William Wilson.

" Isaac Milburn came here as keeper, Thornton succeeded him. They were together for a year or two and Thornton used to tell tales about him. Thornton died in 1900, he was keeper about fifty years up to 1893.[3]

Isaac Milburn lived here at the Dovecot, in a cottage there used to be in the wood.[4] My housekeeper, who came to me

[1] The name of Isaac Milburn, the Portico, appears in a list of Members of Cambo Library in the catalogue of 1829.

The library was established in 1822, and his name does not appear in the catalogue of 1823.

The catalogues were lent by Miss Richardson.

Through the kindness of Miss E. Sheel, Honorary Secretary of the Long-houghton Women's Institute, we are able to add that Isaac Milburn is buried in Longhoughton Churchyard, north of the Church, near the Vicarage Garden. The tombstone is made of rough blocks of marble, with a place in front for the name like a sheet of parchment, and has two or three small sprays of ivy carved, and the following inscription, " A token of gratitude in memory of Isaac Milburn, Bonesetter, who died at Long Bank, January 3rd, 1886, aged 92 years. Margaret, his wife, died 1892. . . ."

[2] Beaten. They were unable to cure her.

[3] Milburn must have left about 1845.

[4] To the south.

when my wife died, lived next door to him over beside Brinkburn somewhere, where he was living when he was sent for to London. It was a great preparation for *Isaac to go to London;* he had to have a new walking-stick made; her father dressed it for him, he was a woodman.

It was a young lady he went to, they were always very quiet about who she was. She hadn't walked for nearly a year. There were several black-coated doctors in her room. Isaac looked at her hip, and then he told all the doctors to go out of the room. He told them very brutishly; they didn't want to go, and the young lady didn't want them to go. So Isaac took up his stick and began to put on his hat. Then she told them to go out of the room; and he put the hip in; and called the doctors back; and she walked across the room. He had found out it was the joint.

I saw Isaac once at Morpeth station, wearing a long hat, and a lot of ladies round him, and he was keeping them all laughing, and I asked who it was. He was twice married. My brother lived beside him at Long Bank, Longhoughton, where he died. He lived in a lot of places. He was alive after I came here thirty years ago.

They do say he attended royalty.

When he lived at Throp Hill, there was a wheelwright next door to him, and he had a stack of *cart felloes*—pieces of wheels—drying, and these kept *disappearing*. He came to Isaac about it. " I'll soon find out who's taking them," and Isaac bored a hole in one of them, and put some powder in, and next day there was a fireplace blown to pieces! No doubt then who'd taken them! "—Mr. William Embleton.

The London story is told also by Mr. Isaac Perceval:

It was " a rich lady " who sent for " the great north country bonesetter, and several doctors and physicians had come to meet him, and they looked out of the door, and saw an auld man with a plaid and a stick coming up the street," and when he came to the door, he asked in the broadest Northumbrian,—" does sic and sic live here, and was it here that somebody was ill, and wanting him? " And he wouldn't have any of them go upstairs with him, " only two women." When he had put the lady right he told her to get up and walk,—" Get thysel' up," and she said she couldn't,—" Ye'll *hae* to,"—" he was that sort of man he spoke the same way to everybody,"—and he insisted and insisted till she did walk, and then " she was that way excited that she took her gold watch and chain from round her neck, and gave them to him."

" My father used to tell that story—about the watch and chain."—Miss Brown, Newbiggin.

" Do you know the story of the *hare* he had in the public-house at Elsdon? He had her on the table, squalling for her life.[1] He worked on with her, and patted her, and set her on her legs on the table, and she was *away* out of the window! "—Mr. Isaac Perceval.

Mr. Isaac Perceval gave an idea of the quickness, as well as the skill, of Isaac Milburn by describing an incident which he himself saw. Mr. Isaac Perceval's father put his shoulder out, when building a wooden hovel; it was Isaac Milburn's day in Morpeth, so he drove his father in at once; when they got there, Isaac Milburn was away to the station, and when they reached the station the train was just coming in. " He just whooped his knee under father's shoulder, and put it in and gave him a bat[2] on the outside of the arm as the train came in,—' Gan awa' hame, ye're a'richt.' They knew each other well. And nothing more was ever said about it as far as I've heard."

[1] Mr. Perceval showed, with his hands, that all her legs were out of joint, so that she was helpless and couldn't get away.
[2] A blow.

CHAPTER XV

" My grandfather lived at the Close House; he attended on
Lady Wilson of Wallington, when she drove out with her
pair of donkeys. He had a coat of special colour, so that she
should know him in the gardens or anywhere. There was
a road then from Wallington New Houses to Middleton road
end, but they used to plough it up. Lady Wilson would wait
till the corn was up, and then she would drive right through
it, to show that she knew there was a road there. Sometimes
you could scarcely see her for the corn.[1]—Mr. R. Adam
Wilson.

Mr. Wilson adds that " she drove there on purpose to keep
the road open." The road went out north of the plantation
at Middleton, on the west side of the road from Middleton
Bridge to Grange Moor, on the top of the little hill, at the
second gate north of the turn to Middleton Station.

Sir Walter Trevelyan was well known as an earnest
temperance reformer. He put down all the public-houses on
his Somersetshire and Northumberland estates. He did not
use the Wallington cellar which was left to him. During
Pauline Trevelyan's lifetime she used to buy wine for
Wallington guests out of her pin-money. Sir Walter left
the Wallington cellar to Dr. Richardson to be used for
scientific purposes. The Executors, who tasted the wine,

---

[1] According to Hodgson, II, I, p. 264:—John Trevelyan of
Wallington, Esq., married in 1791, Maria, daughter of Sir Thomas
Spencer Wilson, of Charlton in Kent, Baronet. Her mother, Lady
Wilson, is said to have been a good deal at Wallington.

say that it had almost all of it gone bad, except some sherry[1] and liqueurs, which were unsurpassable. Sir Walter supported the Whig party in the county. One year he undertook to give the Whig banquet at Alnwick for the farmers and other adherents. Unfortunately he only provided water and lemonade to drink. The Whigs lost the next election.

(N.B.—In 1892 I attended a Liberal banquet at Hexham to celebrate the return of R. MacInnes. There were three hundred present and no one asked for alcoholic drinks. Times change!)—Written by Mr. Charles Trevelyan.

" I was in the house at Wallington, a housemaid, when Sir Walter and the second Lady Trevelyan were there. Lady Pauline was the first Lady Trevelyan, she was very delicate, and they were always abroad a great deal; nine months out of the year; she died abroad, and it was the law of the land that ' Where the tree falls there it must lie,' so she is buried there.[2]

I'm seventy-six years of age. I've been a widow thirty years and had seven children."—Mrs. Pearson.

[1] Compare Chapter XII, p. 106. Sir Walter Trevelyan, Lady Wilson's grandson, owned Wallington from 1846 to 1879.

[2] Pauline, Lady Trevelyan, who died in Switzerland in 1866, was a friend of Ruskin's, and in her time, and with Ruskin's advice, the walls of the hall at Wallington were decorated with pictures by William Bell Scott, by Pauline, Lady Trevelyan herself, and by other artists, but these pictures, though alluded to later, need not be described, as there are full accounts of them in Tomlinson's " Guide," p. 262, and in a printed guide kept at Wallington.

CHAPTER XVI

ANDRA PEARSON, PENINSULAR VETERAN; AND THE MEN WHO FOUGHT AT WATERLOO

Mrs. Pearson has given the following account of Andra Pearson, who fought in the Peninsular War. He was her husband's father.

" He was bound to a weaver; the weaver was a hard man, and he thrashed him; Andra thought nobody should have thrashed him, and he ran away from home to the town.

There they drugged him, and he took the shilling, and they put him on board a ship, and he was away fifteen years, and was in the fighting. When he came back he had his loom, and Sir Walter [Trevelyan] said he could have the bit of ground behind Bent House, if he would clear it; he was a good gardener, and had fruit trees, and that's where they lived.[1] Andra never smoked and never drank. When he was seventy Sir Walter made him write his life, and they sent it to Edinburgh, and it was printed. We had a great many copies, but we've given it, and lent it, and have none left. It's fifty years past January since he died. I'm seventy-six years of age."

" He was in the Peninsular War, and he used to tell us youths about Badajoz and Salamanca."—Mr. George Handyside.

Mrs. Hedley is a granddaughter of old Andra Pearson, and she and her daughters borrowed, from one of her brothers, a copy of Andra's long and detailed autobiography for the Editor to read, and explained some points in the book.[2]

" My father, Andra Pearson, was born at Donkinridge;

[1] Compare Chapter IV, pp. 40, 54.
[2] " Autobiography of Andrew Pearson, a Peninsular Veteran," 1865, published by Lang, Rollo & Robinson, Edinburgh.

old Andra must have lived there before he went to Benty. Andra was a mole catcher, and it would be that way he worked for Mr. Clennell; he lived all those years at Benty, not at Harbottle. Grandfather was such a gardener, and he had the garden beautiful with flowers, back and front, and apple trees; people came a long way to see it. No, I don't know about him building Benty—it was an old house; they were the last people that lived in it. Yes, it was black thatched.[1] After he died, and the back row at Cambo was rebuilt, his widow was offered and accepted a better house, and died where Mrs. Walker now lives. Grandfather could keep people entertained for hours. There were two rooms, and he had his loom in one. I've seen it. Mrs. Handyside here got linen woven by him. Each child had enough for a set, bolster and pillow-cases. I don't know where he got his materials. I used to go up there to tea every Sunday. When he got old he used to shout for my father all day, ' Andra, Andra, Andra,' you could hear him far away from Benty. Granny had a cousin to live with her in Cambo after he died, and it was the cousin gave me one of the towels he had woven. Grandfather wasn't fierce as they've made him in the picture at Wallington—' The Spur on the Dish '—they've just made him like that for the picture.[2] Sir Walter used to get the men to put on all sorts of funny clothes to be painted. How they used to laugh over it."

" My Mother had three brothers at the battle of Waterloo; two of them came safe home, but one of them died after the battle, when crossing the Blue Mountains; they didn't know where that was, but Mr. Henry Codling found out afterwards that there were Blue Mountains." The men were taken for the Army by conscription, Mrs. Hepple thinks; " they wanted my Father too, and he had to seek his register to prove his age. My Mother's family were eleven in number. Sometimes they paid another man to go instead of them."—Mrs. Hepple.

[1] The site of the house and garden is still known as Black Benty.
[2] This reference is to one of the pictures by William Bell Scott, dated August, 1858. Mrs. Thomas Hepple has a photograph of Andra Pearson, which was taken about the time the pictures were being painted. It was given her by Miss Perceval, whose mother, Sir Walter Trevelyan's sister, had it taken.

Old Mrs. Kell, the daughter of a former gamekeeper at Wallington, lived at Bent House and died there about twenty years ago, in her one hundred and second year. As a boy, I used to shoot rabbits in that neighbourhood and sometimes I brought her one as a present. She would gratefully accept it, but on one occasion she shook her head and said: " Ah, you ought to have seen the way my father used to shoot. When he went out, he always took his gun, a stout stick and his snuff-box, and when he saw a bird, he first planted his stick firmly in the ground, then he took a pinch of snuff, and then took aim and always killed the bird."—Written by Mr. R. C. Trevelyan, author of " The Bride of Dionysus," etc.

CHAPTER XVII

KIRKWHELPINGTON AND OTHER PLACES

" There was a string band at Kirkwhelpington Church; they sat in the balcony, which there used to be at the back of the Church. The fore-elders of the Charltons of Kirkwhelpington played in it. There's a story that one sexton asked for estimates to whitewash the Church yellow! "—Mr. Edward Keith.

Kirkwhelpington is a village two or three miles to the west of Cambo.

In the days gone by, the following story was told about a cow-dealer, Luke Cowney, who had bought a cow and was returning home late at night, coming through the churchyard at Morpeth. He had a great habit of talking to himself, and was saying aloud, " There is £5 in her," when he was seized upon by some men and got a great fright. They thought he had been body-snatching, which was done in those days. He shouted out " I am deeing nee harm. I am only auld Luke Cowney the cow-jobber." The house is still standing in Morpeth Churchyard where they watched for the body-snatchers.—Written by Miss Brown, Newbiggin. Her father used to tell this story.

Mr. John Tate of Bank House, near Acklington (in north Northumberland), died on " Carling Sunday, 1832. He was buried at Brainshaugh, and for three nights after his funeral, the old coachman, Jack Anderson, and the watchdog, paced the chapel-yard to watch his grave; for Burke and Hare were then in the habit of stealing corpses and selling them to hospitals for dissection."—His great granddaughter, Mrs. H. G. Carr-Ellison, gives us these particulars from her copy of Mrs. Apperley's typewritten book.—" Memories of the Tates."

119

My father was taught by Mr. Hodgson, who wrote the history of Northumberland; he used to teach them their catechism in the church porch at Hartburn.[1]—Miss Brown.

" There was a blacksmith here, who was bad friends with the schoolmaster, Mr. Sinton, and at church when the schoolmaster got up to play the organ, the blacksmith said—' Thou Son of Saul, Sinton's physogum is the token of defeat,' and walked out.

That was told by Mr. Wardle of the Corridge, who died 1921, at eighty-four years; he was schooled here."—Dictated by Mr. William Wilson.

[1] Hodgson was Vicar first of Kirkwhelpington and later of Hartburn. Hartburn is a village two or three miles east of Cambo. In those days Cambo was in the parish of Hartburn.

CHAPTER XVIII

IRISHMEN IN NORTHUMBERLAND; AND THE GIBBET

" They used to hire the Irishmen in Morpeth on a Sunday, first thing when they came over. A farmer would hire a dozen or eighteen. You had to get either grey coats or blue coats, if you had them both they fit.[1] A've seen a dozen fights at Meldon. If you saw them kissing all round, next thing was a fight! "—Mr. Isaac Perceval.

" The Irishmen at Thropton[2] used to fight with sickles after cutting the corn, and the blood used to run, but they would be quiet as soon as the priest came; they always sent for him to stop them."—Miss Murray.

The Gibbet.[3]

When I first came to Wallington, about 1886, there was a Mr. Potts at Harwood Head, a magnificent borderer, well over six foot high, who shouted out his stories as if he were talking in a hurricane, but really because he was very deaf. He used to say that all the tramps who came over the road asked for the story of the Gibbet. All English and Scotch tramps always commented, at the end of the story of the hanging and gibbeting of Winter—" Serve him right." The Irish tramps always said, however, " Poor fellow! Poor fellow! "—Written by Mr. Charles Trevelyan.

There was a young man passing the Gibbet one night, going to see his sweetheart. As he went by he said " Ha' away wi' us, man! " [4] and there was a man lighting his pipe behind the Gibbet, and *he* answered—" Wait till I get my pipe lit! " The young man took to his heels!—Mr. Hugh Thompson, now of the Dovecot, formerly farmer of Ottercaps farm, which runs up to the Gibbet, on the march[5] of three or four landlords.

[1] " Fought."
[2] Thropton is near Rothbury, about fourteen miles away.
[3] See also Chapter XXIII, p. 162.
[4] To Winter.
[5] Boundary.

CHAPTER XIX

OLD Anderson of Rothley Shiel used to be a shepherd on the Cheviots. He said it was a very lonely life, and he never saw a soul all day, unless he and another shepherd arranged to meet and " try a fall " (wrestling). He died about 1907 or 8.—Written by Mrs. Charles Trevelyan.

Mr. R. Adam Wilson has a beautiful old copy of Robert Burns' poems, illustrated with engravings by Creswick and others, which he bought over fifty years ago under the following circumstances:

He used to drive cattle in to Newcastle Market for his uncle, a distance of about eighteen miles. He was looking at books on an old bookstall, and took out this one,—at once the old Jew rushed up—" You must buy dat, dat good book, spend your money on dat! " but asked some big price for it. " I only had 4s. 4d. in my pocket, I had my bait[1] carrying, but I had to spend a shilling on something else, so I said " Man, I'm only a butcher's lad, and I've only 3s. 4d.; I'll give you 3s. and keep 4d. for myself, and I'll have to walk home." The Jew was furious—" You want to rob me! " And the lad went away to another stall, and took up a copy of Shakespeare, and was thinking of getting it,—and almost wishes now he had! But the old Jew beckoned furiously to him to come back; and the end of it was, that the lad, who had begun buying cattle at the age of sixteen, got his Burns for 3s. 4d.;[2] it has been a life companion and he has refused, again and again, to part with it.

A man was driving a flock of sheep along the road near

---

[1] Food a man carries with him.

[2] Mr. Wilson is a great judge of collies as well as of books. He began exhibiting at the age of sixteen.

Bavington[1] when this [piece of meteorite] fell on the road between him and the drove of sheep. It was in the middle of the day, and the sun shining, and he saw it coming down on fire. He sent the dog on after the sheep, to set them on a bit, and stood still himself, not knowing where it would fall; and it fell between the drove of sheep and himself, and sank into the road. If it had fallen on the other side of the dyke,[2] on the soft ground, it would have been buried. The whole piece he got, was about the size of that flower-pot.[3]   Mrs. Stephenson, the man's mother, gave this bit to Mr. Wilson. Mr. Wilson weighed his piece, which is about half the size of a woman's fist, and it weighed seven ounces. It is rough and yet shiny, and feels very heavy compared to stone.

Mr. Wilson himself saw a piece fall, at seven a.m., in North Northumberland, near Bamburgh, but failed to find it.—Mr. R. Adam Wilson.

" About the year 1894 Mrs. Taylor in Belsay Village, who was then over eighty years of age, told me this story:—When she was a little girl her father was a hind at one of the Harwood farms; a great snowstorm blocked the roads and gateways and no one was able to get to the farm or away from it. Both the farmer's wife and the hind's wife were expecting babies, and the only other woman was the servant girl at the farm. The hind's wife went to bed, and the farmer's wife came and sat beside her, and gave directions to the girl. All went well, and a week later the farmer's wife went to bed. The farmer and the hind carried the hind's wife across to the farmhouse in an armchair, and she sat beside the farmer's wife. It was a fortnight later that the doctor, rather anxious, got through the drifts, and both women met him at their doors with their babies in their arms; ' he was *so* pleased,' said Mrs. Taylor."—Miss Elinor Middleton of Belsay Castle.

Mr. Hugh Thompson, and his mother, Mrs. Robert Thompson, aged eighty-nine, lived for years at Ottercaps. The winters were severe in those days. Twenty-two years ago a young shepherd lost his life in snowdrifts, going from

[1] Just outside our district.
[2] A stone wall, hedge or ditch.
[3] A seven or eight inch pot.

Shilla Hill to Otterburn after visiting the girl he was engaged to. The spot is marked by a stone, about one and a half miles on the Otterburn side of Ottercaps.[1]

A previous year, one of Mr. Hugh Thompson's hogs (year old sheep) lived for three weeks under the snow, she was in what we call a dum hole,—a hole in a limestone country caused by the water siping[2] away,—and she had got a little heather to eat, but she had begun to chew her wool. She did die that winter later on. There were other cases of sheep, told in the paper, that lived far longer under the snow,—forty days or so. To get to his sheep he had to walk right over the tops of the dykes; " the snow was only eighteen inches deep perhaps when it fell, but the drifts were as high as the top of this house "; there were no landmarks to be seen, even the burn was covered, and he could only by chance find the burn, where the sheep had got drifted up. Mrs. Thompson made the tea out of snow; there was no water for the kettle. For thirteen weeks the carrier could not get through, and sledges were used instead of carts, and the sheep lived on hay. A gang of men from Elsdon, and a gang of men from Kirkwhelpington worked to meet each other; they cleared the road nine times, but each time, before traffic got through, it got drifted up again.—Mrs. Robert Thompson and Mr. Hugh Thompson.   Ottercaps is just outside our district.

At an Institute Meeting the following facts were given:—
There were great snowstorms here in 1886, 1888, 1900, 1904, 1910.

In 1886 Mr. Keith walked on the hedge from Wallington to Cambo, and never knew it was there. " There was a snow wreath, outside your house,[3] fourteen or sixteen feet deep."

Mr. Henderson of the Temperance Hotel, Scots Gap, said a train was snowed up there nearly a week. Most of the passengers got away somehow, but we had the platelayers to

---

[1] " I well remember Mrs. Telfer's distress on learning he had left her house in the early hours of the morning, unknown to the family, to return to his charge. He had waited hoping the storm would abate."— Mr. Edward Keith.

The inscription on the stone is " W. S. Carr, found dead on snow, February 13th, 1900."

[2] Soaking.

[3] The Two Queens, at west end of Cambo.

feed.   The wind started in the south-east and worked round to the north-east, which made the drifts very bad, drifts from two directions.[1]

In 1888 it was nearly as bad, the men out of the gardens cut roads for a month.—Mr. Edward Keith.

" I saw three engines, with a snow plough in front, coming down the line; they nearly got through, but finally the men had to dig."—Mr. John Henderson.

In 1910 the line was again blocked, and Mrs. Trevelyan had to walk twelve miles, through deep snow, to get back to Cambo from Morpeth.

[1] Perhaps it was of this occasion that I was told stories before I came to Cambo; a couple from a distant part of Northumberland were snowed up at Scots Gap, and described how fortunate it was, that there were rabbits ir the train, which were commandeered.—R. E. Bosanquet.

CHAPTER XX

PIPE TUNES, SONGS AND DANCES

PIPE TUNES

SIR JOHN FENWICK
(From R. E. Bewick's collection)

THE WAY TO WALLINGTON
(By Rev. Walker, 1857)

THE WAY TO WALLINGTON

(From R. E. Bewick's collection)

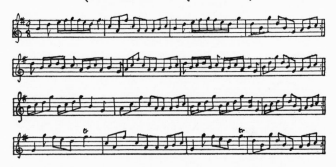

1 Oh canny man, oh shew me the way to Wallington,
  I've got a mare to ride and she has a trick of gallopping,
  I have a lassie beside that winna give over her wallopping,
  Oh canny man, oh shew me the way to Wallington.

2 Weel or woe betide I'll hae the way to Wallington,
  I've a grey mare of my ain that never gives o'er her gallop-
      ping,
  I have a lass for-bye, that I canna keep frae wallopping,
  Oh canny man, oh shew me the way to Wallington.

3 Sandy, keep on the road, that's the way to Wallington,
  O'er the Bingfield Kame, and by the banks of Hallington,
  Thro' by Bavington Ha', and on ye go to Wallington,
  Whether ye gallop or trot, you're on the way to Wallington.

4 Off like the wind he went, clattering on to Wallington,
  Soon he reached Bingfield Kame and passed the banks of
      Hallington,
  O'er by Bavington Syke, the mare could na trot for galloping,
  Now my dear lassie I'll see for I'm on my way to Wallington.

" These stanzas, with several others of a similar description,
were composed by —— Anderson, a Miller of Wallington,
who hunted with his landlord, Mr. Blackett, upon the above-
mentioned grey mare. On rent days, Anderson, who was a

good piper, used to go with the other tenants to pay his rent, but not with money—for taking the pipes under his arm, he struck up and amused landlord and tenants with his favourite tunes and songs, the whole day long, which ended in his getting a receipt in full for his rent, with which he returned home, singing in triumph to his little grey mare," see Chapter XI, p. 103. This note, and the tune of Sir John Fenwick and " Shew me the way to Wallington " from R. Bewick's collection, and " Shew me the way to Wallington " as taken down by the Rev. Walker were found in manuscript at Wallington, written down during the days of Sir Walter Trevelyan, who died in 1879.

The other three versions of " The Way to Wallington " were privately printed at the suggestion of Sir Charles Trevelyan, who died in 1886.

Mr. T. Leighton was one of the Harnham family.   Cf. Chapter IV, p. 62, and Chapter XXII, p. 153.

Mrs. Arkle was for thirty-five years schoolmistress at Cambo. She died in 1886 at the age of sixty-seven.

Dr. Collingwood Bruce was the great authority on the Roman Wall.—Mary Trevelyan (Mrs. Charles Trevelyan).

SHEW ME THE WAY TO WALLINGTON
(*Mr. Thomas Leighton's version*)

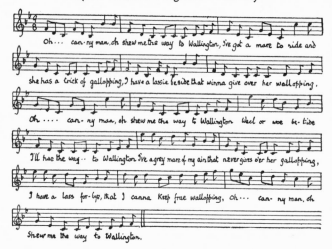

Oh... can-ny man, oh shew me the way to Wallington, I've got a mare to ride and
she has a trick of gallopping, I have a lassie beside that winna give over her walloping.
Oh .... can-ny man, oh shew me the way to Wallington Weel or woe be-tide
I'll hae the way .. to Wallington I've a grey mare of my ain that never gives o'er her gallopping,
I have a lass for-bye, that I canna keep frae walloping. Oh... can-ny man, oh
Shew me the way to Wallington.

Shew Me the Way to Wallington

(Dr. J. Collingwood Bruce's version)

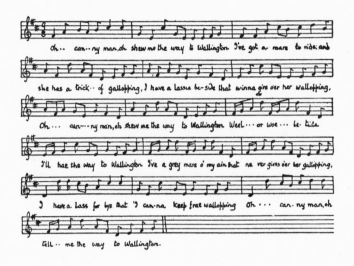

Oh.. can...ny man, oh shew me the way to Wallington I've got a mare to ride, and she has a trick.. of galloping, I have a lassie be-side that winna give oer her walloping, Oh... can---ny man, oh shew me the way to Wallington Weel... or woe... be tide I'll hae the way to Wallington I've a grey mare o' my ain that ne ver gives oer her galloping, I have a lass for bye that I' can-na keep free walloping Oh... can ny man, oh tell.. me the way to Wallington.

The Way to Wallington

(Mrs. Arkle's Version)

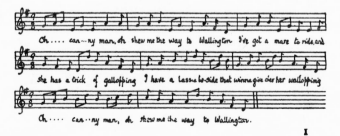

Oh.... can...ny man, oh shew me the way to Wallington I've got a mare to ride, and she has a trick of galloping I have a lassie be-side that winna give oer her walloping Oh.... can...ny man, oh shew me the way to Wallington.

I

CHILDREN'S SONGS

RISE SALLY WALKER

Rise Sally Walker, Rise if you can, Rise Sally Walker and choose your good man.

> Choose to the East and choose to the West,
> Choose to the very one that you love best.
>
> Here is a couple married with joy,
> First a girl and then a boy.
>
> Seven years after, seven years ago,
> Now is the time to kiss and go.

Sally stands in the centre, the other children walk round her. She chooses one, and takes him into the centre. At the end of the song they both go back into the circle of children and a new Sally comes into the centre.—Mrs. Batey, Dovecot; Miss Davison, Harwood Gate.

THE JOLLY MILLER

There was a jolly miller and he lived by himself. As the wheel went round he made his wealth, One hand in the hopper and the other in the bag, as the wheel went round he made his grab.

Couples dance in a ring round one, the Miller, who stands alone. At the words "He made his grab" each man lets go of his lady, and seizes another partner, while the Miller also tries to get a partner. The one who fails to secure a partner becomes Miller in his turn.—Mrs. Batey, Dovecot.

WE ARE THE ROMANS

Have you any bread and wine? We are the Ro-mans. Have you any bread and wine?

We are the Ro-man sol-diers.

2 Yes, we have some bread and wine,
   We are the Normans.
   Yes, we have some bread and wine,
   We are the Norman soldiers.

3 Will you give us some of yours?
   We are the Romans.
   Will you give us some of yours?
   We are the Roman soldiers.

4 No, we won't give any of ours,
   We are the Normans.
   No, we won't give any of ours,
   We are the Norman soldiers.

5 Let us join and have a ring,
   We are the Romans.
   Let us join and have a ring,
   We are the Roman soldiers.

The children stand in two lines holding hands, and advance
in turn as each side sings a verse. At the end they all join
hands and dance round in a ring.—Miss Wales.

THE BIG SHIPS

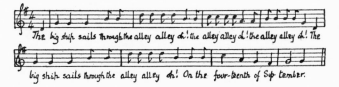

The big ship sails through the alley alley oh! the alley alley oh! the alley alley oh! The

big ship sails through the alley alley oh! On the four-teenth of Sep-tember.

Two children take hands and form an arch—the other
children run under the arch in a long line again and again.—
Mrs. Dicks (who was Miss Davison, Low Fairnley); Mrs.
Batey.

In and Out the Windows

In and out the windows, in and out the windows, in and out the windows, As we have done before.

2 Stand and face your lover (*bis*)
As you have done before.

3 Follow me to London (*bis*)
As you have done before.[1]

The children stand separately in a circle: one child goes in and out during verse one.   In verse two she faces her lover. In verse three she races her lover, and the one who gets back to the vacant space first returns to the circle, whilst the other goes in and out.—Miss M. Truelove (now Mrs. W. Robson).

The Wind Blows High

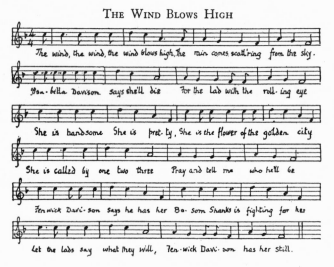

The wind, the wind, the wind blows high, The rain comes scatt'ring from the sky.

Bon-bella Davison says she'll die For the lad with the roll-ing eye

She is handsome She is pret-ty, She is the flower of the golden city

She is called by one two three Pray and tell me who he'll be

Fen-wick Davi-son says he has her Bo-som Shanks is fighting for her

Let the lads say what they will, Fen-wick Davi-son has her still.

Mrs. R. Davison has put her two children's names into this song—she said " The girls and the lads like to hear their names put together: Bosom Shanks?[2]   Oh, I don't know

[1] Appendix C.
[2] Compare Heslop, " Northumberland Words." Buzzom, a besom or broom. Shanks, legs. Buzzom-shanks, a broom handle. Buzzom is also an expression for a simpleton.

who that is—we always used to say it like that. The children stood in a circle and danced round while they sang. —Mrs. Charles Trevelyan.

WE ARE THREE JEWS

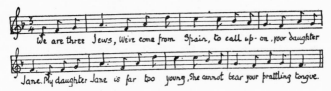

We are three Jews, We've come from Spain, to call up-on your daughter Jane. My daughter Jane is far too young, She cannot bear your prattling tongue.

2 The naughty girl she won't come out,
   She won't come out, she won't come out,
   The naughty girl she won't come out,
   To help the ladies dancing.

3 The pretty girl she has come out,
   She has come out, she has come out,
   The pretty girl, she has come out,
   To help the ladies dancing.

The children stand in two lines, one child is picked to pull a child from the opposite side; the side which gets most children wins.—Mrs. Batey.

SALLY GO ROUND THE MOON

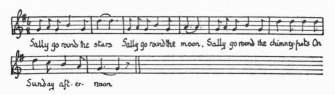

Sally go round the stars Sally go round the moon, Sally go round the chimney-pots On Sunday aft-er-noon.

All the children dance round in a ring, for instance round the maypole.—Mrs. Truelove.

Oh, bonny Tyneside

—Mr. John Batey, Dovecot, Cambo; music taken down by Mrs. C. Trevelyan.

Oh, bonny Tyneside, shall I see thee once more,
After long years of exile away from thy shore,
Thro' far foreign countries a rambler I've been,
And much have I suffered, and much have I seen,
For I've been in a land where a brighter sun shone,
Yet ne'er saw a country as fair as my own,
And I never have seen in my wanderings wide,
A spot I loved better than Bonny Tyneside.

Oh, bonny Tyneside, I come weary and worn,
How few are the friends left to greet my return,
I'll away to the hills, and I'll wander all day
Along the green banks where the lambs are at play.
The poor silly sheep with their tracks o'er the fells,
The bonny wee birds with their nests in the dales,
But a home and a hearth I've yet to provide,
For I'm now but a stranger in Bonny Tyneside.

Oh, bonny Tyneside, where my infancy passed,
Like a beautiful dream 'twas too happy to last,
I see the green fields where in childhood I strayed,
And the school green at Wall where so often I played;

The Schoolmaster still in the village is seen,
The schoolchildren they are at play on the green,
But the schoolmates I knew, they've gone far and wide,
They have wandered away from Bonny Tyneside.

Oh, bonny Tyneside, my darling lives there,
She waits on my coming her love to declare,
Since the day that we parted, she faithful has been,
And the wide ocean lay like a barrier between.
She's as fair as the morn of a beautiful May,
As bright as the eve of a midsummer day,
How happy I'd be with her as my bride,
And a snug little cottage on Bonny Tyneside.

—Taken down by W. G. Whittaker, D.Mus., Newcastle-upon-Tyne, from Mr. James Batey, the Orchard, Kirkwhelpington, and inserted with their kind permission.

Mr. John Robinson thinks it was written about sixty years ago, and that the writer had been to Australia.

It is known to a good many of our members and their relations—for instance, Mrs. Robinson and Mr. Edward Keith. Mr. William Embleton, Mr. and Mrs. Batey (Dovecot), Miss Mary Wales, Miss Truelove, Mr. Edward Pearson.

Dancing

Cambo people have always been fond of dancing, and have danced whenever they could get a room.

" At the first flower show at Cambo I was three years old; it was held where your vegetable garden is now, on the bleaching green. Mr. Gow was newly married, and he said to my father, ' Now, Matthew, you take my wife, and I'll take ——,' and they led off the Keel Row, and at the end Mr. Gow clapped his hands, and said, ' Well done, Matthew ! ' "—Mrs. Pearson.

The Cumberland Reel.

To any six-eight tune. Longways for as many as will. Progressive.

The first couple, taking right hands, walk down the middle to bottom, and back again, skipping step to places. First couple casts off, man to the left, woman to the right, followed by all the other couples, to bottom, where first couple form an arch. The other couples come through the arch (sk. s) and without stopping, take both hands across and skip up to top. Here they cast off to the left, still holding hands across, and followed by first couple, who have by now dropped their arch. All dance down to bottom, and up to top again, the second couple now becoming first couple, and the original first couple becoming last couple. So on, till each couple has led in turn.—Mrs. Charles Trevelyan.

PART IV

ANCIENT MONUMENTS AND PLACE NAMES

CHAPTER XXI

IMPLEMENTS, CUP AND RING MARKINGS, EARTHWORKS

In the original suggestions in *Home and Country* for the "Best Institute Book," we were asked, amongst other things, to collect information about "Ancient monuments and legends or superstitions connected with them." In this, as in other details, we understood that we should "get local tradition, excluding what comes from strangers and from books." Thus, our point of view is still folklore. We write of what interests us because it touches our daily lives. We do not deal with all the old remains which are mentioned in books, or in maps; this is not a local history. We are like the boy in the fairy tale, dropping our crumbs, or our white pebbles, so that those who come after may see by what road we have travelled.

We have not many legends except those given in Chapter VII about boggles. Some of our ancestors attributed all mysterious earthworks and roads either to the Romans or to the Devil. To-day antiquaries are inclined to take away a good deal from the Romans as well as from the Devil, and to connect many of our early earthworks with races of men before the Roman conquest of Britain. Those who wish to be certain of seeing Roman work should go to the Roman Wall, to the forts on the line of the Wall, and to the road near it; or they should explore the forts on the line of the Roman road past Woodburn and High Rochester; or they should visit the Department of British and Medieval Antiquities in the British Museum, and see a silver vessel and the ornamental handles of other silver vessels found in Silver Lane, Capheaton, in 1747, which are thought to be plunder from a Roman sanctuary or temple, perhaps on the Tyne, about two hundred years after Christ.[1]

The word "camp" is misleading. Many so-called "camps" are not camps in a military sense,—many are prehistoric villages or forts, thousands of years old; some are probably stells or nightfolds, and may be much more recent,—wolves and bears as well as men were always a danger to sheep and cattle; some may be survivals of a forgotten system of cultivation of the land.

IMPLEMENTS

"My wife's brother, Hedley of Elf Hills, found a spear sticking out of the runner[2] down yonder near Prior Hall."—Mr. George Shade.

Mr. Ephraim Hedley's sons say their father was in the field with the lambs, and saw something glittering and pulled out the spear. He went and told his master, and word reached Wallington Hall, and they dug, and found bracelets. It was to the east of Prior Hall.[3] Mr. Ephraim Hedley is now the farmer at Elf Hills.

[1] Article by Rostovtzeff in "Journal of Roman Studies," XIII (1923), p. 99 ff. with Plate V.

[2] "Runner, a small stream."—Heslop.

[3] A letter from Sir C. E. Trevelyan to Dr. Bruce, August 23rd, 1880, gives an account of the find on May 14th, 1879. "Arch. Ael.," 2nd ser., Vol. IX, p. 52, with coloured plates.

This is one of many hoards of bronze implements, which are our chief source of information about the development of civilization in early times. It consists of:—four leaf-shaped spear-heads (one having "protected loops"), three armlets, three swords, fifteen axe-heads, eight of which are palstaves, deeply flanged, and seven are socketed axes. Bronze began to take the place of stone implements about 2000 B.C., and iron in turn replaced bronze about 500 B.C. Such hoards were often buried by travelling smiths; they may include old pieces collected for melting down and new ones ready for sale. Comparison of many such finds show how types were gradually improved. The Wallington find belongs to an advanced stage but not the latest. The swords are still rapier-like, meant for thrusting, a type which was succeeded by the leaf-shaped cutting sword; the latter began to reach England from the Continent about 1200 B.C., but new fashions were slow in reaching Northumberland, and the form of the axes suggest a rather later date

CUP AND RING MARKINGS

On *Tod Craig,* Ottercaps, on the Ray Estate, there is a rock with cup and ring markings. A hollow like a cup with two circles round it, measuring about eleven inches across, occurs four times. There is one cup with a tongue and two incomplete circles, about thirteen inches in diameter; two or more with one circle visible; eight or more with no circles. With the help of Mr. and Mrs. E. R. Newbigin and Mr. H. L. Honeyman three tongues in all have been made out, but no ducts. The markings extend over a rock surface of ten foot by five foot.

Similar incised stones are found in many parts of the world. They are generally near important " camps " or burial places, and objects found in the barrows lead to the belief that cup and ring markings date from the bronze age.[1]

for the Wallington hoard,—perhaps 1000 B.C. The implements do not show the degree of uniformity that would show they were from one mould, and some of them were probably worn before they were buried, which would suggest that they may have been somebody's property, and not the stock of a travelling smith. Besides their use as tools and weapons, they were a portable form of wealth.—Mr. R. C. Bosanquet, Rock Moor, author of " Borcovicium."

Mr. Parker Brewis has referred to the hoard in his article on " The Bronze Spear-head in Great Britain and Ireland," " Archæologia," 61, Part II, p. 463, and in his article on " The Bronze Sword in Great Britain," " Archæologia," 73, p. 256, and plate xxxvii, fig. 13.

The hoard may be seen at Wallington.

A socketed axe, a stone mould and a bronze shield boss found on the Wallington estate are in the British Museum. The stone mould has depressions for two flat axes of Early Bronze Age type on one side, and for one such axe and a ring on the other. It had been found in a field a little to the north of Cambo, and was presented by Sir Walter Trevelyan in 1852. The socketed axe from Greenleighton is in the Greenwell collection, as is also the bronze shield boss. The axe is of the Late Bronze Age. The shield boss was found at a spring, Harwood. It resembles those of the Late Bronze Age round bucklers.

From information kindly supplied by Mr. Reginald A. Smith of the British Museum, and his assistant, Mr. C. Hawkes. " Arch. Ael.," IV, p. 102. Paper by Ed. Charlton.

[1] In a barrow, opened by Mr. R. Cecil Hedley and Mr. W. Percy Hedley of Corbridge, at Ouston, near Stamfordham, in 1928, the cover stone of a cist was incised in this way. " This burial," Mr. W. Percy Hedley says, " was probably a beaker age burial, of the early part of the bronze age." A smaller cist had " a very fine cup mark on the inner face of a side stone." " Proc. Soc. Antiq. Newcastle," 4th ser., III, p. 257.

At Tod Craig the markings were protected by grass which covered the rock. Some years ago in a very hot summer, the grass was scorched up, the sheep lay on the rock, and kicked away the turf, and these markings were laid bare. We are indebted to Dr. James McCracken and to Mr. Kenneth McCracken for showing them to two members of Cambo W.I. So far as we know there are not any important earthworks close by, though there are mounds which may be barrows to the east or south-east.

" In a lecture by Mr. D. D. Dixon at Cambo years ago, he pointed out how the ancient Britons told the time of day by the sun on the rocks. There on the rocks on Rothley Crag are these round places."—Written by Miss Mary Murray.

Miss Mary Murray took two of us to see the holes in the rocks, which she had noticed; they were similar to those on the Punch Bowl rock at Shaftoe Crag, and also near the edge of the crag. See Chapter XI, p. 105. I have consulted Mr. D. D. Dixon. He does not know these particular holes in the rocks at Rothley and Shaftoe, and he no longer thinks that cup and ring markings were used to tell the time; they were probably connected with some worship. Possibly the holes at Shaftoe and Rothley may originally have been cup and ring markings greatly enlarged by centuries of exposure to the action of wind, rain and loose fragments of rock.[1]

BARROWS

" *Brian's Hill* was opened by Dr. Greenwell in Sir Walter's time, and an urn was found.[2] It is where the stone wall takes a turn in the West Wood," [at Wallington. It is west of the large gate which is opposite the Well House.] —Mr. Edward Keith.

[1] Later I examined a well-known specimen of cup and ring markings on a rock at Lordenshaws, and observed that, beside the cup and ring markings, there was one pot-hole on it, which had presumably been enlarged by nature from a cup and ring made by man. Close by was a smaller piece of rock with cup and ring markings, which had split off from the main block.

[2] Sir Walter Trevelyan died in 1879.

Mr. George Handyside's uncle, Mr. Richardson, was farming Broom House when Sir Walter Trevelyan opened the mound in the field beyond Broom House, and found urns and bones. It was to the right of the path going to Kirkwhelpington. There is a heap of stones there now. The field belongs to the Capheaton Estate.—Mr. George Handyside.

The field is called " the Broom," but is part of the more distant farm of Fawns.[1]—Miss M. Wales.

There was a place on *Salters Nick*, at Shaftoe Crags, where Mr. Isaac Perceval was digging once, when he came on bones and big round stones. The bones all went to dust. He reported it, and there was some talk of excavating there, but nothing was done.—Mr. Isaac Perceval.

" There was *a long grave* at the end of Catmire Wood, [Rothley], which Pearson, the keeper, dug out. It must have been for a very big man. There were some bones left. There were stones. Pearson was always finding some old thing.—Miss Murray.

" The *Standing Stone* by the side of the south end of the China Pond at Wallington is a companion to the similar stone by the tumulus on Shaftoe; they were known as ' Poind and his man,' [2] it was brought from Shaftoe to Wallington."—Written by Mr. G. M. Trevelyan.

Hodgson (II, I, 348, 349) was told that Sir Walter Blackett brought it from Shaftoe.

When complaints were made, one of his successors expressed his willingness to give it back, provided the complainants would come and fetch it, but they never did come for it. Such is the story as handed down in the Trevelyan family and remembered by Miss Pauline Trevelyan.

[1] Mr. W. Percy Hedley tells us that he opened a barrow on Fallowlees in 1926, which contained a burial after cremation; that Dr. Greenwell opened one at Greenleighton (his No. 212), and also one at Fawns, which contained urns and burials after cremation (Greenwell, " British Barrows," p. 433).

[2] The name was in use in 1552, when the watch had " to be kept at the Two Stones, called the Poind and his Man, with two men nightly of the inhabitors of Bollame." Nicholson's " Border Laws," pp. 282, 302. The name implies a tradition which seems to be lost. Poind in Lowland Scots means " a silly, inactive person," Heslop writes, quoting Jamieson's Dictionary. The stone was removed after 1718, when Warburton described the two large standing stones and the trenches between them. Hutchinson's " Northumberland," II, p. 284.—Mr. R. C. Bosanquet.

" Camps "

" There is a camp on *Crow Wood hill*, south of the wood. There are trenches and a deep place in the middle; if you lay down nobody could see you." [1]—Miss Mary Murray.

Her sister—Miss Murray—mentioned the camp round *Ewesley Station*, immediately to the north, outside our district. [2]

Mr. Edward Keith in Chapter XI, p. 105 has referred to a " camp " on *Shaftoe Crag*, and to the discussion about the holes in the Punch Bowl Rock near it.

In a paper read before the Newcastle Society of Antiquaries on 29th March, 1922, by Mr. Thomas Ball, this " camp " is described as one of a series of " forts " on and near Shaftoe Crags. The next " fort," he mentions, is at a point which will be discussed again in Chapter XXVII— *Salters Nick*. In this " fort " there are traces of a number of *hut circles*. There are about nine " forts " and " camps " in that bit of country, round Bolam, Angerton and Shaftoe, which he describes. " Proc. Soc. Antiq.," 3rd ser., Vol. X, pp. 237-250.

Mr. John Robinson tells us that " the oldest town in the country is Lordenshaws; it is near the road to Rothbury; you can see the places where the huts stood." [3]

" In a lecture at Cambo Mr. D. D. Dixon described Lordenshaws as one of the most perfect ancient British camps in the district."—Mr. Edward Keith.

In the blacksmith's field, north of the exhibition field, and north-east of *Close House, Cambo,* are three long mounds, with deep hollows between them.

Mrs. Edwin Pearson, wife of the postman, says that when gathering sticks there with an older resident, she was told, " This was where the soldiers used to hide."

---

[1] Crow Wood is on high ground to the east of Rothley Crag; the hill rises steeply beyond Rothley Park Farm. I do not think this is " the camp," on " Beacon Hill," described by Hodgson, II, I, p. 306; perhaps that is identical with another " camp " pointed out between Rothley Castle and Rothley village, marked by a solitary tree. These are only pebbles dropped, in the hope that an expert will follow our steps some day and put us right.

[2] See " Proc. Soc. Antiq. Newcastle," 4th ser., Vol. I, p. 234.

[3] Eight or nine miles from Cambo.

Miss Emily Charlton says that " as children we always called them ' the camp holes.' We used to play soldiers and bombardments there for hours. There are holes too just over the stile from Close House,[1] and they used to be much deeper, but when these houses were being built they tipped the rubbish there."

It is often discussed what these were,—Mr. Keith says that Mr. Nixon, the former estate agent, thought they had been claypits, but they may have been fortifications.

Mrs. Charles Trevelyan thinks they are the heaps from coal pits, and says Mr. Nixon thought there had been coal workings under Cambo front field adjoining the blacksmith's field, and that the ground had subsided.

Mr. Henderson, Scots Gap, says that in his hayfield, at the west end,[2] there is a trench [near the gate of the field, leading on to the cart road from " the Pant Gate " to the Saugh House. The Pant Gate is explained in Chapter XXVII.]

There are traces of a camp in a field to the east of *Wallington New Houses*. The ditches are shallow.[3]

Manside Camp, or Gunners Box.

" The right name is Manside Camp, Gunners Box is just what we call it. It'll be because it's the place where the warriors lay. It is a large square enclosure with a deep trench all round. There'll have been a lot of fighting up there. There are a lot of graves—heaps of stones on Hemmel Hill, a mile or more to the north-east. The Antiquaries came and opened them in Sir Walter's time, but they found nothing much." [4]—Mr. George Shade.

---

[1] Hodgson, " History of Northumberland," Part II, Vol. I, p. 329. " Besides the camps already noticed in this parish, there is . . . a third, east of the Close House, a little within the march of the Morpeth Ward, circular, but much defaced of late years by the plough." He also speaks of a " circular " camp " on the Deanham ground on left bank of Swildurburn and the east side of the road to Capheaton."

[2] I think this is not the field referred to by Mr. Handyside in Chapter IV, where there was a colliery; I think that was farther east.

[3] Hodgson calls it " somewhat rectangular and oblong," Part II, Vol. I, p. 329 footnote. See " Proc. Soc. Antiq. Newcastle," 4th ser., Vol. I, p. 174. Paper and plan by Mr. T. Ball.

[4] In the Ordnance Survey it is Manside Camp. It is known locally as Gunners Box. The Editor wondered whether it were Gunnar's Box, like

"In Sir Walter's time they used to make a point of lunching there; there was a spring below it. The name might come from that. Manside Camp will be the real name."— Mr. James Thornton, nephew to the late Mr. Thomas Thornton.

[This camp is far more conspicuous than the one at Wallington New Houses. The ditches are far deeper and it is in a commanding position, on the moors between Greenleighton, Harwood, Elsdon and Otterburn.]

The base of a cross stands at one corner of Manside Camp.—Mrs. Charles Trevelyan.

The Trevelyan family always call this a Roman camp.[1]

Gunnarton, and Gunnar Heugh and Gunnar Peak Camp. See " Arch. Ael.," 2nd ser., Vol. X, p. 12, and Tomlinson, pp. 211, 212.

Mr. Thomas Thornton, who was keeper at Wallington for forty-nine years and nine months, and was under Sir Walter, lived with Mr. Shade at Harwood Gate for a time after he had retired. This camp is described by Hodgson, II, I, p. 288, but he gives it no name.

[1] Mr. W. Percy Hedley has pointed out that " it was at one time considered that all rectangular camps were from their shape of Roman age, but it has since been shown that many camps of this shape are British in origin. The presence of a camp . . . far from a Roman road would tend to suggest that it was British." He adds that in the " Survey of the Debateable and Border Lands in 1604," edited by R. P. Sanderson, Alnwick, 1891, p. 85, the name is " Mann's Head Crosse."

Possibly the socket stone of the cross may at one period have been used to bear a gibbet from which a skull or wooden model of a man's head hung, or a gibbet may have stood beside the socket stone as is the case at Winter's Gibbet; both are on the boundary of the ancient lordship of Redesdale.

" Every free manor or barony had its own gallows, and the sites of many of these are now preserved in the numerous Gallowhills found all over the county " (Chapter XXIV, p. 169).—Mr. W. Percy Hedley.

Mr. R. C. Bosanquet thinks it " quite possible that it was a Roman fort, built to hold a small detachment for some time; the ditches are too big for a temporary or one day camp. Such small forts usually had one gate " [as this one has]. He compares it " with the tiny Maiden Castle on Stainmore (150 ft. by 120 ft. to centre of ramparts), a stone fort built astride a Roman road, with three different hollow-ways intersecting or skirting it (" Cumb. and Westd. Trans.," N.S., Vol. XXVII (1927), p. 170 ff.). Probably the fort (and cross) were landmarks on a medieval route, used perhaps by raiders who would find the ditches a convenient shelter. On a bare moor any conspicuous feature serves as a fixed point and may ' attract ' the road."

On Thomas Arkle's map, in his " Statistical Account of the Parish of Elsdon," a road is marked which leads " to Morpeth," from Elsdon by Whiskershiels to the corner of the parish over the boundary of which Manside Camp lies; he does not mark the camp or cross.

The Fawns.

It is often said that there is a Roman camp at the Fawns. There are large and puzzling earthworks within a stone's throw of the present farm. Antiquaries have difficulty in forming an opinion as to their origin. They may be of later date than the Romans. "There was a little peel-house or bastell here" at the time of the survey in 1541.[1] The farm stands alone now in fields, but there was once a road past it.

"The Roman Road." "The Devil's Causey."[2]

"I knew an old man at Hartburn, who had dragged the chain when they were making the Ordnance Survey, and he

Additional camps are: West Shank, Doddhouse and Combhill, all near Greenleighton—Hodgson, II, I, 329.

There is a small Roman enamelled bronze cup or bowl in the British Museum, in the same case with the Capheaton silver; it has "the remains of blue and green enamel in leaf design." It was "found in a ploughed field at Harwood," and given by Sir Walter Trevelyan in 1852. It had been found some years before, and is presumably the same mentioned by Hodgson, II, I, 274, "a small, but very antient enamelled copper cup, found near Harwood." Engraved in "Arch. Ael.," IV (1855), p. 102. Paper by Ed. Charlton. See "Guide to Antiq. of Roman Britain," B. Museum, p. 95.

I am indebted to Mr. Reginald A. Smith, of the British Museum, and his assistant, Mr. C. Hawkes, for information they have about it.

[1] Hodgson, II, I, p. 195.

See "Proc. Soc. of Antiq. Newcastle," 4th ser., Vol. I, pp. 224-228. Plan and Paper by Mr. T. Ball.

[2] Hodgson, II, I, 301; H. MacLauchlan, "Eastern Branch of Watling Street," 1864, p. 10; "Proc. Soc. Antiq. Newcastle," 4th ser., Vol. II, p. 104.

The main Roman road through Northumberland into Scotland ran from Corbridge to Woodburn, up Redesdale to High Rochester, then over wild moorlands by Coquet-head to a great fort on the Tweed at Newstead, east of Melrose. A mile or so north of the Roman Wall a less important road, which we call the Devil's Causey, branched off north-eastwards. It has been traced for fifty-five miles by way of Hartburn, Brinkburn, Bridge of Aln and Lowick to the mouth of the Tweed. Its paving and lay-out were typically Roman. It may have been constructed at the time of Agricola's conquest of North Britain, to maintain communication with a fleet operating on the east coast and using Tweedmouth as a base. Clearly it soon became obsolete, for there is no sign of re-metalling (such as gradually raised the level of roads that were long in use) and no permanent forts were built to guard it.—Written by Mr. R. C. Bosanquet.

said they could tell it through the ploughed fields by the stones that were turned up. I knew a man called Codling at Hartburn, who told me it passed through the ford there: you can tell where it crosses the Hartburn road; yes, " the Harpeth " it's called there.—Mr. Edward Keith.

CHAPTER XXII

" THE TROUBLOUS TIMES "

OF the period of Saxon, Norman, and Early English we can point to few " monuments." Something of our history in those days can be read, by those who understand, in our customs, in our place names, and in the names of the members of our Institute.

A series of stone grave-covers of about the Crusading period are preserved in our modern Church at Cambo, having been brought from the site of the old chapel on Chapel Hill.[1]

The bases can still be seen of medieval crosses—Manside Cross and Steng Cross, which mark the boundaries of the lordship of Redesdale.[2]

PELE TOWERS AND HOUSES

The Pele Tower at Ray.[3]

Mrs. Wilkinson of Hartington was partly brought up in it; when she lived there her friends had a room on the first floor, and the cows were still driven in below. It was very old-fashioned built, much more so than the Cambo fortified house, —thick walls, and holes show how they barred the door, a stone staircase outside. It was thatched.

The Pele at Cambo.

The village shop is a square house with walls four foot thick, ground floor, and two stories above. Before 1818 a

[1] Hodgson, II, I, pp. 282, 283, with illustrations.
[2] Chapter XXI, pp. 143, 144.
[3] Ray is outside our district, but as the tower has now been pulled down, and the walls are only a few feet in height, it is worth recording what we know of it.

shop had been kept on the first floor (compare the story of the
warlock in Chapter VI, p. 82), which perhaps indicates that
the place into which the sheep and cattle were driven at the
bottom had not been converted into a room or rooms until
1818. Mr. George Handyside says there was an iron door, and
an outside staircase; of the latter no trace remains. Some of
the stones of the lower part of the building are of great
size.[1]

Hartington Hall, a square, solid, three-storied house, with
thick walls and the remains of at least one old open fireplace,
is probably much the same—save for the enlarged windows—
as it was in 1541 when it was called " a strong bastell house
of the inheritaunce of Sir John Fenwyke in good reparacons."
Stories still hang about it of Meg of Meldon, the wife of
Sir William Fenwick, who lived at Meldon and at Hartington
Hall, and was said to go backwards and forwards between
the two places, by an underground passage, which came out
near the Knocking Stone. We owe this information to Mrs.
Charles Trevelyan, and to Miss Hall.

" When I was a child, we were afraid to pass the bridge
over the Wansbeck, because she used to sharpen her knife
there. It was a stone bridge, and was all worn down as if
knives had been sharpened. No, it's not the bridge near
Northside. I was never feared to pass that one; it was the
other bridge, and the old one; it's not there now." [2]—Miss
Ann Elizabeth Robson.

" She is still supposed to haunt a lane near Whalton;[3] they
don't like passing through it."—Mrs. Keith.

" My grandfather was lighting his pipe at a bridge at
Meldon, and kept striking the flint; and he heard a horseman
coming; and the horseman halted; and my grandfather went
on striking the flint; the horseman waited till he saw the
striking again, and then he thought he'd seen enough, and
turned round and fled! My grandfather thought he'd tell
people he'd seen Meg that night! [4] This story is quite an

[1] See Frontispiece by Mr. Robert Marshall.
[2] Meg of Meldon was well hated for her meanness. The bridge
described was near Meldon, some miles from here.
[3] Whalton is also some miles away.
[4] For other stories of Meg, see Chapter VII, p. 88; Hodgson, II, I,
p. 287; " Denham Tracts," II, pp. 244-253; Raine's " Memoir of
Hodgson," II, p. 255; M. A. Richardson's " Table Book Leg. Div.,"
Vol. I, pp. 135-141.

old one. I never saw my grandfather, and I'm sixty years of age."—Mrs. Davison, Low Fairnley.

" *Low Fairnley* is an old *pele tower*, the sheep and cattle were driven in at the bottom."—Mr. George Charlton. Confirmed by Mr. George Handyside.

The house, occupied by Mr. and Mrs. James Davison, is reached by a flight of old, irregular steps: the walls are three foot thick in both stories, and are made with clay instead of lime, as Mr. Davison knows, having helped to concrete them inside against damp.

" There was a spy hole[1] to see the Scots coming." There are two rooms on each floor. There used to be a third floor. " They've taken a storey off, it used to be all thack;[2] my husband helped to take the thack off." The mantelpiece in the kitchen was nailed to the ceiling when they came, and before that again there evidently had been an old open fireplace, they could tell where it had been. " The door was black, and the cheeks[3] were white."

The door of the house " has no cheeks," and " is hung as a gate would be "; the bolt runs into the wall, and there are metal pieces across the door.

Over the doorway is

W.B.B^{t.}

1723[4]

Under the house is a large space, used now as an implement shed, into which, it is always said, the cattle were driven to be safe from the Scots; it was used as a byre till a short time before Mr. and Mrs. Davison came, then it was condemned on account of scarlet fever, and the door was enlarged to admit implements. In the implement shed there are traces of two small windows; the one is very rough, a slit, splayed with huge, unhewn stones, which would have faced out where the steps now are; the other is square, and similar to the small windows in Cambo pele, and also to the square windows in a lean-to at Low Fairnley, where a family used to live, but which was not part of the original building, and may have been added in the nineteenth century. The interior of this bottom

[1] At the north side of the kitchen.
[2] Thatch.
[3] " " Cheek, the side of a place; ' the door cheek.' "—Heslop.
[4] The last Sir William Blackett.

part of the pele is composed of the largest and roughest stones, which on the south side seem to bear traces of fire, as does also the exterior west end wall, but here there had evidently been other buildings, and Mr. Davison has been told that there were.

There were also a " lot of houses on the other side of the burn." [1]

Mr. and Mrs. James Davison, have helped with this description.

" *Another Pele Tower is Ottercaps.*" [2]—Mr. Hugh Thompson.

" *The Beacon Hill,* near Greenleighton, above Longwitton Station. On this a beacon was lighted to give warning of the Reivers before the Union." " The foundations of the hut are still visible on the hill." These facts were mentioned at an Institute Meeting by two of our visitors, husbands of members, and by Miss McCracken. " There are still remains of the watch tower."—Mr. Edward Keith.

The old metal beacon is still in existence under cover at the Wallington Gardens.

" Beacon grates " they are called by Mr. Walter Hedley.

" There is a *Keep at East Shaftoe.*"—Miss Shanks, Cambo.

This Keep is a magnificent, vaulted hall which, Miss L. Robson tells us, dates back to 1264. A winding stone stair originally led up to a watch tower, and traces of it can still be seen in a corner of the hall, and in a similar recess on the floor above. The south front of the house has the appearance of a Manor house, but appears to date from three periods; a pointed doorway leads straight into the vaulted keep in the earliest part, and a square doorway forms the present chief entrance. The walls are three to four and a half feet thick almost all over the house. There are beautiful mantelpieces decorated with scallop shells.

The Aynsley arms appear on an old grave-cover stone,

[1] In 1552 " the tenants of Ferneley " were ordered " to keep a watchman nightly about their own houses."—Nicholson, " Border Laws," p. 274.

[2] This building is used for farm purposes but is no longer inhabited. Outside our district—the farm is the scene of Mr. Hugh Thompson's snowstorm story. Chapter XIX, p. 124.

unearthed by Lady Decies in 1840, which is now built into
the end of a farm building. It is a very large one, double,
evidently for husband and wife, showing both sword and
shears, and is illustrated and described in the 1901
publication of the Newcastle Society of Antiquaries after a
visit to Shaftoe.[1]

Tradition had preserved the memory of the site of a chapel
and enabled Lady Decies to discover the tombstone beneath
the turf.

The site is amongst the bracken, after passing through a
gate beyond farm buildings. Miss L. Robson has taken part
in digging there, and uncovered part of an old pillar, " and
three steps leading up to a recess where an image might have
stood. One can easily gauge the dimensions of the chapel,
and its greatest length, sixty-six feet from east to west, was a
common feature of old churches. The burial-ground from
which Lady Decies unearthed the stone is south of the church.
I have not heard of any description by Lady Decies of her
activities around the Church site, but where I was digging
the earth had been previously disturbed." [2] Miss L. Robson
pointed out that the family of Shaftoes took an active part in
Border warfare. In 1575, at the Raid of the Reidswire, on
Carter Fell, were heard the battle-cries of " a Shafton! " and
" a Fenwick! "

" *New Deanham* is an old farmhouse."—Mr. John Robinson.

The abstract of the articles for building this place, dated
1669, and quoted by Hodgson, II, I, p. 295, are such an
accurate description of New Deanham Hall as it now stands,
that little description need be added. The stone staircase is
now within the house instead of outside. The original outside walls are from three to five feet thick. The front door
has a " Tudor " arch, and above it is a sundial with the
date 1670, and decorated with dog tooth ornament; there is a
similar arch, with hooks for a strong door, opening on to the
staircase from the first floor. The old open fireplace in the
hall was altered when the present tenants, Mr. and Mrs.
Buglass, came. There is a fireplace, in one attic, of the same
period as the doorways, finished at the side with a little carving,
—probably a leaf or a flower.

---

[1] " Proc. Soc. of Antiq.," Vol. X, p. 66.
[2] See also " Arch. Ael.," 1st ser., Vol. II, p. 412, for a letter from
John Hodgson dated 1831.

RUINED VILLAGES

Great Bavington.

" I have heard my grandfather say that Great Bavington
was burnt by the Scots; he said that in the troublesome times
as they travelled they burned; he had been told by his fore-
elders. It was a large place once; you can see where the
houses were on the crag as you go in." [1]   The speaker, Miss
Shanks, lived as a girl with her grandfather who farmed
Kidlaw, near Great Bavington. The family came originally
from Scotland, *much* more than one hundred years ago,
—perhaps two hundred years ago.   They settled first at
Catcherside, afterwards at Thockrington, which is near Great
Bavington. Her grandfather died in 1870 in his eighty-second
year.

Harnham.

There is one village in the neighbourhood still in existence,
which shows us what these ruined villages may once have
been. It is in the district of Belsay Women's Institute, but
we are tempted to poach as Harnham is the old home of our
member, Mrs. William Wilson, and the present home of some
of her family. It stands like an Italian hill town, or like
Bamburgh Castle, on a high crag.   " You can see it has been
made for fighting, nobody could get up the rocks at the back."
—Mrs. Wilson.

Harnham Hall, occupied by Mr. and Mrs. Wake, is similar
to a south country manor house in front.   Hardly any
very old houses have survived in Northumberland except pele
towers and castles.   And this house, with its three-foot
thick walls, its dog-toothed doorway, and old fireplaces, has
perhaps only come down to us because of the precipices, steep
slopes, walls and gates which protected it and the little village.

---

[1] Great Bavington is a few miles outside our district.   Compare Chapter
VII, p. 87 footnote.

Before the Union there were few houses of stone except peles.   The
wooden huts with turf roofs were easily burnt and easily rebuilt.   Where
you have the visible foundations of a village of stone houses, it seems
more than probable that that village grew up after 1603, when James I
united the Crowns of Scotland and England.   The borders never really
settled down until the effective Union of the Kingdoms, in 1707, opened
a new era.—From a note by Mr. R. C. Bosanquet.

The back of the Hall faces north and is built on the very edge of the crag, so much so that the kitchen windows are not made to open, because it would be too dangerous. On the little walled terrace are the places " they used to shoot through," and at the back of the house roof, with its ornamental chimneys, is a fierce little tower commanding wide views. Standing there in 1922 some of us felt very near to " the troubled times."

It was Mrs. Wilson who took us to Harnham. Other details can be found in guides and old histories, but only a long visit can reveal all the old associations,—almost every doorway in the onstead[1] showing the date and initials of some Leighton, or other owner in the eighteenth century.

The following account of some of the villages, around the Cambo Institute district, was given by an old builder and mason on the spur of the moment.

Bolam was an old village but none of it is left. It must have been burnt down. There are ashes where the mounds are. My father used to say that when excavating, on the site where the village used to be, they found a lot of burnt timber and stone. He died thirty-three years ago, and was over seventy when he died, and he went to Bolam as a young man, so it was probably seventy years ago these things were found. They say there were three saddlers' shops.[2]

Thockrington and *Great Bavington* are other ruined villages. *Kirkwhelpington* is all newly built. There is nothing left of *Whelpington*. Kirkwhelpington and Whelpington were both old villages.—Mr. John Robinson, who lived at Bolam as a boy.

West Whelpington is one of the largest areas easily traced of a deserted village; it has been strongly protected, artificially and naturally [being on an outcrop of whinstone, steep on the north and west, and steep on the south with the Wansbeck at the bottom]. The easiest way to get to it is by Cornhills, on the road to Sweethope. [It is south-east of Cornhills.] —Mr. Edward Keith.

The village was deserted long before Hodgson's time, 1827, but when the present Mr. Robert Thornton's grandfather,

---

[1] Group of farm buildings.
[2] The Rev. R. E. Thomas, who came to Bolam in 1888, could remember the last house of the old village, between the church and Bolam Hall.

Mr. Robert Thornton bought Cornhills, in 1857, from various owners (a Dodd, a Winship, a Lamb, etc.), some of the walls of West Whelpington were still standing, and he led stone from there.[1]   Mr. Thornton says that some of the area is divided up into half acre strips by remains of old fences, just as to-day in Kirkwhelpington the Duke's cottages each have half an acre; the position of the cockpit can be traced beside a single tree.

Middleton used to be a much larger village—round the present village, between Todridge and Middleton, besides the traces of another village on each side of the road south of Middleton, which are mentioned by Hodgson in his History of Hartburn Parish.[2]—Mr. Edward Keith.

There are also indications as of old houses in a large field to the west of Middleton Hall.

As to the site south of Middleton Bridge Mr. John Robinson remembers a house which there used to be near Middleton Bank Top. He thinks it used to be a blacksmith's shop, though he cannot remember it as such.[3]

" The old men used to tell me that the old village of *Cambo* was on the other side of Wallington Bridge, south of the bridge and east of Deanham; there are mounds there.[4]

There was a village at *Greenleighton* near the wood, also at *Fallowlees*." [5]—Mr. Edward Keith.

Mrs. Charles Trevelyan says there is a ruined house at Fallowlees which looks like a pele.

Longwitton has the grass-grown mounds of old houses along the roadside, and must have been a " long " village, whereas

[1] " My grandfather used to ride his pony every week to Newcastle Cattle Market in the early morning, sell his cattle, and ride home again at night,—Newcastle being twenty-four miles away. He always wore a top hat, and over his overcoat his checked plaid—he was never without his plaid."—Mr. Robert Thornton.

[2] They were grass-grown stones even in Hodgson's time, and he offers no explanation, but a document he quotes indicates it was in existence in 1635.—Hodgson, II, I, 313.

[3] The old coaching road ran over the bridge past Middleton Bank Top.

[4] A large amount of living or working has evidently taken place on the site referred to between the Wansbeck and Old Deanham; there is a very long line of mounds.

[5] It is said that Greenleighton once had a population of one hundred, now there is the farmhouse and one cottage. In 1541 there was " a little stone house with a barmekyn," " Arch. Ael.," Vol. XIV, p. 46. A barmekyn was a strong outer wall. Fallowlees consists of one house occupied by a shepherd.

now there are only a few isolated houses. The reason suggested for this in Murray's handbook, edition of 1860, is that after the Union of England and Scotland in 1603, people, who had hitherto lived in villages for safety, went out to live on the farms.

It will be observed that some of the reasons most frequently given in writings on social and economic history for the decay of villages have not been mentioned by our contributors, though perhaps implied in Chapter IV.

One of the reasons for the decrease in population in the last hundred years is briefly explained by the words— " when the tillage went, the people went "; but it must not be assumed that the disappearance of one village necessarily meant a decrease in the population of the district. In some cases it is clear that a new village was built to which the inhabitants of the old village moved. Belsay is said to have taken the place of Bolam, and many of the inhabitants of the old village of Rothley[1] seem to have moved to the improved or new houses at Cambo, at the Dovecot, and at Close House when the water supply was found inadequate. Even the reader at a distance may notice how many of our older authorities come originally from Rothley.

" There is, or was, a bit of *Rothley Castle*—the old castle— close to the road leading to Rothley village, on the left as you turn up to Rothley; there was much more when I first remember it. It was behind the malt kil'; undoubtedly it was a bit of the foundations of a very large building, but there were only about two square yards left, and there was a well [between it and the malt kil']."—Mr. John Robinson.

He came to Cambo from Gallowshill, Bolam, thirty-five years ago. He speaks of the present artificial ruin, called Rothley Castle, built in the eighteenth century, as " the new one." Are the foundations he describes the remains of " *Rothley Tower*," which in the Survey of 1541 is called a " lytle towre," " in measurable good reparacions "? It had been built by the Abbot of Newminster. Hodgson, II, I, p. 307, and note on p. 306.

Newminster Abbey is close to Morpeth, and we pass its ruins as we go in to our market town.

Miss Ann Elizabeth Robson mentioned a *subterranean*

---

[1] See Chapter IV, p. 61; Chapter XXIV, p. 166.

passage from Stannington to Newminster Abbey.   One of those present doubted stories of subterranean passages, and Miss Robson replied with a story of her own childhood,—of a boy who had escaped from Stannington Reformatory by one, and came out at the conduit at Springfield.   " I remember well Mr. —— hid him in the cupboard, it might have been here [between window and fire], and they came in to look for him, and he was there all the time.   I peeked[1] at him through the crack; and he kept him there three days and let him go when they were gone, but they got him afterwards. He hid him because it was his parents' fault, they had neglected him, and so he was put in a reformatory.   There are some who have had the care of children, who should be put in reformatories theirsels, and if I had had a vote I would vote against them.   That was sixty-four years since.   I am seventy-one."

Miss Robson's mother found a great many coins on the banks of the Wansbeck at Newminster Abbey where she was stoning the land.[2]   There were silver coins amongst them like 6d. or 1s., and a little silver spoon, but only the copper is left.   They include the coins of many foreign countries; there is a French one of 1792 with the head of Louis XVI, and the cap of liberty.

[1] Peeped.
[2] Taking stones off the land.

CHAPTER XXIII

THE EIGHTEENTH CENTURY

AT the end of the seventeenth century the Blacketts came into possession of the Wallington estate, and rebuilt Wallington Hall; in 1728 Sir Walter Blackett inherited the estate, and proceeded, up till his death in 1777, to supply the landmarks, " monuments," roads, and houses which were lacking.

" Wallington " has been fully dealt with in two articles in *Country Life*, June 22nd and 29th, 1918, by Sir George Otto Trevelyan, but we will give here a few fragments of old tradition which are not included in that account.

Cellars, underground passage and " the Arches " at Wallington.

A story, which comes in later, of an underground passage from Rothley Castle—was mentioned to Mrs. Pearson; she had never heard of it though she used to play there as a child.[1] " There was an underground passage from Wallington—from the cellars—to a place in the parks between the house and the Wansbeck. There were horses always kept ready saddled in the cellar."—Mrs. Pearson, and her son, Mr. Edward Brodie Pearson, quarryman.

" It was that way, that—wasn't it a Blackett that was executed?—got away, but they got him afterwards. It was one of the Blacketts, or one of the Fenwicks. It was then that they put up the Triumphal Arch; it was down there then."—Mrs. Pearson.

In the foundations at Wallington, which are the remains of " the strong toure and stone house," mentioned in the

[1] Page 160.

survey of 1541, there is one cellar which Sir Charles Trevelyan used to say must have been the stable of the Fenwick house.—Mr. Charles Trevelyan.

Mrs. Keith remembers her grandfather puzzling over this question of the position of the stable.

The level of the ground has obviously been much raised artificially round the present house at Wallington.

Sir John Fenwick, who sold Wallington in 1689 to Sir William Blackett, was executed in 1697 for his connection with Jacobite plots. Fenwick had been in danger of arrest for some time before he actually was arrested in the south of England.

Sir William Blackett—the son of the Sir William Blackett who bought Wallington, was in 1715 suspected of Jacobite sympathies, and was apparently fleeing from both the government and the Jacobites in the same year.[1]

The parents of the present Cambo schoolchildren have believed firmly in this tradition or legend of the underground passage and have directed me to the exit near the Wansbeck, up which the boys used to venture. By others—who ought to know—I am assured, as one always is assured about underground passages, that there never was one, that this place is only the exit of an underground stream, or a conduit. The fact that this tale of an underground passage is still told of four different places—Shaftoe Crag Cave, Rothley Castle, Stannington and Wallington, shows what a sense of unrest and of secret comings and goings pervaded the neighbourhood two hundred years ago.[2]

There were two sets of *Arches*, one at the top and one at the bottom of a terrace that ran down from Wallington to the Wansbeck. One set has entirely vanished. When Sir Walter Blackett built the Courtyard in 1754 he put up one where the coach house now stands, and ordered a fine iron gate to be made for it. This gate is now in a garden somewhere on the Tyne.[3] Presumably when Sir Walter Blackett found the Central Arch was not big enough for a carriage to drive through, he did not put up the gate, for it was never at Wallington. When he built the Clock Tower he removed the Arches to where they now stand, and had a

---

[1] Hodgson, II, I, pp. 259, 268-270; Macaulay, " History of England," IV, Chapters XXI and XXII.

[2] Chapter XII, p. 106; Chapter XXII, pp. 155, 156, 160.

[3] At Wylam Hall, which belonged to a Blackett, Mr. Keith says.

vista, a grass drive through the east wood from the China Pond. One can see where the grass drive has been, because there are no trees of Sir Walter Blackett's planting in that part of the wood.—Told by Sir George Otto Trevelyan, author of " The American Revolution," to Mrs. Charles Trevelyan.

The Arches stood originally where the Clock Tower is in the Courtyard. As the central arch is not wide enough to admit a carriage, they were supposed to date from the time when most travelling was on horseback. When Sir Walter Blackett built the coach houses and Clock Tower, he removed the Arches and put them in a field south of the Prior Hall, intending to plant an avenue of trees from the China Pond, at the end of which the Arches should stand. This proposed avenue is marked on a map, at Wallington, but was never planted.—Written by Mrs. Charles Trevelyan.

Wallington China Pond.

The carved figures, dragons' heads, and other strange stones are from Aldersgate, London. When the gate was taken down they were brought to Wallington.[1] They are of the period of James I, when the gate was rebuilt or redecorated. In the wood to the east of the Pond, next to the ha-ha on the field side, is a flat bit of ground now overgrown, which was the eighteenth century bowling green at Wallington.— Written by Mr. G. M. Trevelyan.

" I've heard that Sir Walter Trevelyan cut a way through the wood so that he could see the Arches, and through the Arches to Rothley Crag from the wood."—Dictated by Mrs. Thomas Hepple. Her mother used to live in a house, marked on the Ordnance Survey as Bolt House, not far from the China Pond.

Codger Fort was built as a defence, to hold the defile between the two lakes at Rothley against a possible Scottish invasion. There is at Wallington a letter from the Master of the Ordnance at Chatham about the six cannon that were placed on it. A gun was fired when the Lakes were first filled.—Written by Mrs. Charles Trevelyan.

[1] It is said they were used as ballast for Blackett ships coming from London. According to Hodgson II, I, p. 306, they were used to ornament the grounds of Rothley Castle till after Sir Walter Blackett's death.

Rothley Castle and Deer Park.

As one of his enterprises which altered the face of the countryside, Sir Walter Blackett created a deer park at Rothley, building round it a high stone wall which is still in existence. He erected the sham ruins of a castle in the most prominent position on Rothley Crags, a very solid building which still stands with very little dilapidation. *Codger Fort* was built by Sir Walter Blackett after the rising of 1745, when the Pretender's army marched as far as Derbyshire before its retreat. It is possible that Sir Walter, knowing that in 1715 his predecessor had been hand and glove with the Jacobites who rose in Northumberland under Lord Derwentwater, wished to make some unmistakable demonstration of his loyalty. So he built the fort to command the road which was one of the possible lines of advance from Scotland. It was clearly in those days an almost unassailable position if defended by artillery. There are still at Wallington records of payments for ordnance and ammunition for the fort supplied from Woolwich. So it was a serious fortification in its day. The Park was stocked with deer for many years. But when Sir Walter ceased to be a member of Parliament for Newcastle, for which he sat for forty years, the deer were disposed of; apparently they had been preserved mainly to supply venison to the Freemen of Newcastle to keep them loyal to the Blackett connection.—Written by Mr. Charles Trevelyan.

" Rothley Castle and Codger Fort will all have been built as beacons. They used to burn the beacon on Rothley Crags. You used to be able to see from the China Pond to Rothley Crag."—Mr. George Charlton.

" The Castle at Rothley was built in troublesome times. It was built for troublous times, with places for them to hide behind and fire through. Codger Fort, too. No, I don't know whether there ever was fighting there, I'm not much of a reader."—Mrs. Pearson.

" Sir Walter Blackett used to fire from there [Rothley Castle] to amuse himself, I've heard it said, but I won't vouch for it."—Mr. John Henderson.

" We used to be told as children that there was an underground passage from Rothley Castle to Nunnykirk."—Miss Mary Murray.

There is a dark place under the stairs which they never explored. The Castle was a good deal repaired by Mr. Daglish in recent years.

The Rev. C. A. Fitch used to say that Rothley Castle and Codger Fort were built by Sir Walter Blackett at a time of unemployment to give work. He thought he had probably been told this by the late Mr. Henry Codling, or by Mr. James Thornton.

" Rothley Castle, Codger Fort, and the walls of the deer park were built by Sir Walter Blackett at a time of lack of employment; he gave them that privilege, they had a standard wage—little enough in those days—and if they got a chance of another job they could go away to it and come back again when it was finished."—Mr. James Thornton.

Mrs. Pearson was quoted as having said that " a man's wages used to be 10d. a day."

Mr. Thornton replied—" Mr. Henry Codling,—they'll have been there [at Kirkwhelpington or Wallington] for generations—I've heard him say that mason's wages were 8d. a day when the Oakford Bridge was built, and that was about the same time [as the Castle, fort and walls].

There were two deer parks at Rothley; one was from Slatey Ford past Rothley Mill; the wall is there yet, but the deer did not do well for want of heather, and whether they gave that up or put the two together, I'm not sure."

Amongst some manuscripts at the school in the care of Miss Richardson, there is a note:—that £11 5s. was paid in 1744 to Squire Widdrington of Long Horsley for 30 head of deer, and that " in 1752 a bill was paid to William Hadrick for going to Somersetshire for 2 bulls, 2 cows, wild beest, £3 11s.; wild cattle bought from Mr. Trenchard, Abbotsleigh."

" All the farm used to be a deer park, this [Rothley Park Farm] was the house where the man lived who shot the deer. There are cellars underneath where they kept the sherry, ten steps down. The walls of the park are still high. That was Lady Blackett's Drive [a field away to the west of the farmhouse].[1] It joined the main road at the Coach Turns."—Miss Mary Murray.

[1] See also Chapter XXVII, p. 178, for Lady Blackett's Drive and Coach Turns.

Wesley's Tree.

At the Saugh House a stone bears the inscription—" John Wesley preached here on his 70th birthday on June 17th, 1782," and beside it are thorn trees, within an iron railing.

" Cook, the farmer at Saugh House, who was a noted fiddler at all the Barn Dances in the neighbourhood, was so impressed with Wesley's sermon that he buried his violin under the old thorn tree that night, and never played again." [1] —Written down by Mr. Edward Keith from Mr. Henry Codling's stories of old people.

Wesley had been preaching in " Rothbury Forest " before he came here, twelve miles away, and he went on to Hexham, sixteen miles farther on. Mr. Robson of Catcherside's fore-father was at the meeting, also the great-grandfather of Mr. Thornton of Cornhills, who was then at Harwood.—Miss McCracken, and others at an Institute Meeting.

Miss McCracken lives at Saugh House, and thinks she heard about it from Mr. Thornton of Cornhills, the present Mr. Robert Thornton's grandfather.

An open air service is held every year at this spot on the Sunday nearest to June 17th.

This was a revival forty years ago, that is one hundred years after Wesley's service.—Miss Edith Lamb, from her father Mr. Joseph Lamb, Scots Gap.

Miss McCracken remembers that great crowds used to come to it; considerable numbers come still.

Winter's Gibbet.[2]

The story is told in Hodgson, II, I, p. 101. The Gibbet is a conspicuous object on the moors.

" It was my great-great-uncle who arrested the murderer at Throckley Moor when riding on the road to Newcastle, and the family at the Raw still have the handcuffs used. The township was going to fine them £50 if he wasn't

---

[1] " Cambo School . . . had a benefaction of £5 a year, for 20 years, from Mr. Thomas Cook, of Saugh-house, farmer, who died 4 March, 1816; and of £2 10s. a year, for the same term, from his brother, Mr. Jacob Cook, who died 9 March, 1817."—Hodgson II, I, p. 280.

[2] See Chapter XXVII, p. 179.

arrested within three days. There is a barn at the Raw, which was where Margaret Crozier lived who was murdered. She had a shop."—Miss Mary Brown.

Two of Miss Brown's great-great-uncles were amongst the men who went in pursuit of the murderer in 1792. The handcuffs have been shown to us.

Miss Oliver describes the barn as " a pele," there is a little window, and over the window Mrs. Oliver says there is a face carved in stone, and the initial H.

The murderer's name was Winter, and he and the two women with him were gipsies. A boy saw Winter and the women after the murder, and took careful notice of them. It was a cold-blooded murder of an old woman. Winter was hanged in Newcastle, and the body brought back and gibbeted, that is, hung on a gallows, erected at this high and conspicuous spot, as a warning.

" The boy who counted the nails died of consumption, he fretted so, for the two women had threatened him. There were two boys, they were shown two knives, and he recognized one, where the ring goes; it was a sort of clasp knife."—Miss Mary Brown.

" It was the herd lad at Harwood that gibbeted Winter.[1] He was lying there talking to him, and there was blood on the knife; he put a bit of grass in the heft; they showed him lots of knives at Morpeth, but he would have none but this one. And he counted the nails on his boots, and the nails were the same as on the floor of the old woman's house.

The gipsies were cruel to him, so he was taken into the house at Longwitton; if he hadn't had a good horse they would have killed him;—but he couldn't help it, he had to tell. My mother told me about it, and her mother told her; she was at Little Harle at the time. I've never seen anything about it in a book."—Mrs. J. Davison.

" And my father told me," put in Mr. J. Davison.

" My grandmother saw Winter after the murder at Little Harle; he had long black hair plaited, and the women were pulling it ! "—Mrs. J. Davison.

The story of the gibbet has taken as firm a hold on the moors, as the story of the fairies in the more cultivated country.

[1] Gave the evidence which caused him to be hanged.

Yet another account is: " Jimmy Hindmarsh of Whisker-shiel was the boy who gave the information on which Winter was convicted. He was taken as groom at Longwitton Hall, where Perceval the Prime Minister was. The gipsies nearly got him in the avenue, and would have done so if his horse had not jumped the gate at the end. Afterwards he was sent secretly to Perthshire, but he developed consumption there, and came home to die, and they left him undisturbed till the end."

" My grandfather used to tell us the story but we didn't like it."—Miss Shanks.

" When the Gibbet was erected in 1793 it was on the main road to Scotland. There are references to it as a grim object in contemporary records. The chains creaked in the wind. After the bones fell to pieces there was a wooden body and head put up. When I first knew it the old gibbet was beginning to decay. There was the head only hanging, all cut about and pitted with shot marks. In the days of muzzle-loaders, when the only way of unloading at the end of the day was to fire the gun the shooters used to end up at the gibbet and fire at the head.

Sir George Trevelyan erected a new gibbet in 1894, of the same size as the old one with a wooden head hanging. Shade was one of the three men who erected it."—Written by Mr. Charles Trevelyan.

Greave's Farm.

On the right hand side of the road through the fields between Broom House and Kirkwhelpington, in the first field, the ground plan of many buildings can be seen.

Mr. George Charlton says the old men told him that it had been Greave's Farm,[1] held by a man named Greave on the Little Harle estate. Afterwards two farms were put together. He cannot remember it himself.

---

[1] Five children of the name Grieve figure in Robson's list of Cambo scholars before 1805. " Greave's Dean " is marked, not far off, on the Ordnance Survey Map. For Robson's list of scholars see Chapter IV, p. 53.

CHAPTER XXIV

PLACE NAMES AND LOCAL EXPLANATIONS OF THEIR MEANINGS

MOST of the names of our villages and farms in this neighbourhood are very old, indeed Saxton's map made in 1579, in the reign of Queen Elizabeth, contains nearly as many of them as a modern motoring map does.

Cambo is an exception, but though it scarcely seems to be marked in maps until Sir Walter Blackett built or rebuilt it in the eighteenth century, it appears from 1230 onwards in documents.[1]

" Do you know that this place is generally called *Cámma*? It always gets *Cámma* from natives." [2]—Mr. William Wilson.

There was a chorus of agreement when the Institute Committee were asked as to the pronunciation.

One or two other residents have said that education is introducing " Cambo," you hear it more frequently than you did thirty or forty years ago.[3]

Hodgson having been the most accessible book of reference, his quotation from Wallis " the camp on the hill " has been accepted here as the derivation of Cambo, but Hodgson in a later passage comes very near to Professor Mawer's suggestion that it may mean " heel of land where slate (cam) is quarried." [4]

" Bits of Cam from Elf Hill Quarries were used to write on slates, or for marking door steps; they made a yellow mark."—Mrs. Hedley.

Cam used to be sold for the same purpose by women

---

[1] See Hodgson, II, I, p. 278; and Mawer, " Place Names of Northumberland and Durham," p. 38.

[2] The accent is on the first syllable.

[3] In Kitchin's eighteenth century map it is Camma, though Camboe and Cambois are variations in other eighteenth century maps.

[4] Hodgson, II, I, pp. 278, 323; Mawer, p. 38.

hawking things from door to door round Embleton [a village by the sea in Northumberland.]—Mr. Gilbert Telfer.

Mr. John Robinson did not know that Cam was found at Elf Hills, but as it is in small deposits it may be worked out. There is Cam at Kirkwhelpington. Mr. Keith's statement that the old men had told him the site of old Cambo was on the other side of the Wansbeck was mentioned, and Mr. Robinson replied, " Well, there *is* Cam on the Wansbeck at Kirkwhelpington, and it lies that way." [1]

Wallington.

Were there Wallings, and were they Britons? [2]

Wallin*gton*. The " *town* end " is still the word used to describe the road end of what is called " Rothley Village."—Mrs. Hedley.

" Rothley *Town* " it is called on a Wallington Estate map of 1728.

Greenleighton.

The field in which the farmhouse stands is called " the Green." [3]—Miss McCracken, who used to live there.

Rothley Village puzzles newcomers. It was long before the Editor could find it! It consists now of the farmhouse, and three other houses.

" As children we were taught to call it Roadley, now they are taught at school to call it Rothley. There were ever so many houses at Rothley in those days[4]—a shoemaker, and a mason and a shop, all the way up from the road to the farmhouse. Later the house we lived in was condemned, and my father, my mother and my sister moved to Rothbury where they took lodgers."—Mrs. Pearson.

---

[1] Some years ago I had a glimpse of an old map or plan in a drawer at Wallington on which old Cambo was marked as having been between the present village and Elf Hills.

[2] Wealing is a patronymic [or surname] from O.E. wealh, " foreigner, Briton "; Wallington may mean " farm of the sons of the Briton," Mawer, p. 206.

[3] Mawer, p. 133; Hodgson, II, I, p. 288. In documents of 1252 and 1255 the name is given as Litendon, Lightdon, Lutedon. Dun is an old word for hill. Professor Mawer thinks it may originally have been Lightwine's hill. Lightwine occurs as a man's name, in another part of England, in Domesday Book.

[4] When she lived there as a child, Chapter IV, p. 61.

" There were quite a number of houses there, and a cooper when I came to live at Scots Gap, but the quarries and limekilns near Longwitton were closed, and the people went away."—Mrs. Arkle, Scots Gap.

Mention is made by Mrs. Hedley and by Mr. Keith of the number of people employed at Elf Hills quarries and kilns, and of the road they used coming from the Saw Mills, which is near Rothley Village. These quarries and kilns are no longer working.[1]

Mary Castle.

A quarry and an unroofed house are called by this name. Mrs. Pearson was asked why the quarry was so called.

" It was because of *Queen* Mary; she came there once on the quiet, that's what I've always heard."

" Was it a Castle? "

" It was a farmhouse; Sir John [Swinburne] took the roof off because the tramps used to sleep there."

" She came when she was fleeing," somebody else said.

On reading Hodgson II, I, p. 192, it seemed probable that this ruined farm was built shortly before his time, taking the place of a house farther to the south, and was called a Castle because it was " finished with square-headed and embrasured gables "; also that the Mary referred to might be the Virgin Mary; St. Mary's Close, St. Mary's Well, the Lady Lands, the Lady's Yard are all in the same neighbourhood, where Newminster Abbey once owned property.

In spite of this the speakers were firm. " It's handed down."

The modern interpretation of the name Mary Castle, though possibly incorrect, reminds us how near we are to Cap-heaton, from which messages were carried on horseback by the Misses Swinburne, on behalf of the ill-fated Stuarts, in 1715.

THE VILLAIN'S BOG, SCOTS GAP, GALLOWSHILL, REDPATH

There is a group of so-called " camps " and place names, which must be dealt with together as their stories are interwoven.

---

[1] On the other hand quarries are now working at Knowesgate on the western side of our district, and families are living there in wooden houses.

There are two " camps " on Grange Moor farm, which
are marked on the Ordnance Survey, the one to the north-east
of the railway, the other to the south-west. The " camp "
to the north-east has one modest rampart still visible.

The " camp " to the south-west is a bit of broken ground,
with the clearly marked foundations of a small enclosure,
about eight yards by twenty-four yards, and a mound near
with stones showing. This " camp " is marked on the
Ordnance Survey as " The Villain's Bog."

Hodgson, II, I, p. 302, describes " the ancient nightfold
called the Villain's Bog," the robbing of it by moss-troopers,
and their defeat at Scots Gap by the people of the neighbourhood. Compare Mackenzie, Vol. II, p. 160. " Proc. Soc.
Antiq. Newc.," 4th ser., Vol. I, pp. 232-235. Paper and plan
by Mr. Thomas Ball.

At our Institute Meeting, there was some doubt and discussion as to which was the Villain's Bog; two of those
present thought it was to the north-east of the railway.

Mr. George Handyside, whose nephew has the farm, and
whose grandfather knew Hodgson, says—" Yes, they put the
sheep and cattle there to be safe from the Scots. It is just
beyond Middleton Railway Arch on Grange Moor Farm.[1]

When they were building the houses at Scots Gap, they
found a lot of bones, and when we were going to Rothley
we used to be afraid to come past there."—Mr. George
Handyside.

Mr. George Charlton, speaking of boggles,[2] said " there was
one at Scots Gap. They used to walk to the Hirings at
Morpeth, before the railway was made, and somebody always
had to meet them at the Gap for fear of the boggle. But the
trains frightened it away ! "[2]

" Was it a Scotch or an English boggle? "

" I don't know, there was enough Scots and English
killed there for many boggles. And they say the chief of
the Scots was hanged at Gallowshill, and that's why it is
so called. That's what I have always heard."

---

[1] It seems possible that the name Villain's Bog may originally have
been given to the land both north and south of the railway, and even
farther west, and that the original Villains were not the Scots but
honest Saxons (or Northumbrians) holding their land and grazing their
cattle and sheep on the whole Bog, on the terms known as villenage,
under one of the feudal lords.

[2] See Chapter VII, p. 89.

Mr. George Handyside agreed. " Yes, that's what I've always heard about Gallowshill."

On several farms " there are stells or folds with stone walls where they used to put the sheep when the Scots were coming. We were told that there was a hole near Rothley Park where they used to put the sheep, but we've never been able to find it." [There is a legend that the sheep and cattle used to be hidden in the hole where Rothley Lake now is,— the east lake below Codger Fort, which is fifty feet deep in places.]—Miss Mary Murray.

" There were two moss-troopers hanged on the trees at Gallowshill, that's how it got the name. My father and his brother were born in the house in the lane at Gallowshill. Our grandfather's uncle was there before him. Before that they were at Elf Hills. The house in the lane is now used as a hemmel. A hollow in the field behind the house they call the moss-troopers' grave."—Miss Murray.

Mr. Thomas Murray, farmer, Gallowshill, pointed out " the moss-troopers' grave," a low place, in a field between the farmhouse and the house in the lane, which has never been ploughed. He says that his father would have been eighty if he had been alive to-day. His father was born in the present farmhouse; the family had been ten or eleven years at Elf Hills before that, so they must have been nearly one hundred years on the estate. He himself was born at the cottage in the lane which his cousins refer to.

Mrs. George Davison of the Saw Mills, who was a Miss Murray of Gallowshill, mentioned that they had had a spiritualist staying with them, and she said to them when passing the place where the moss-troopers are buried—" Has any bad crime ever been done here? "

The late Mrs. Robert Davison, who was also a Miss Murray of Gallowshill, wife of a signalman, Cambo, said of Gallows-hill, " The moss-troopers were hanged there. There was a man called Ray who tried to save the cattle, and they killed him, and cut him up in the lane.[1] I was born in the house there which is now an implement shed " [previously called a hemmel].

" The old story is that the farmer followed the moss-

[1] The lane is grass grown, it leads from High Hartington to the main north road from Cambo to Harwood Gate, and is probably part of an old road. Compare Hodgson, II, I, p. 286.

troopers to Redpeth, where they turned on him and cut him into collops (Northumbrian for slices)."—Mr. Edward Keith.

The two stories told by Hodgson seem to have run together since his time, his story of the fight at Scots Gap in defence of the Villain's Bog having become merged with that of the robbing of Gallowshill. He does not bring in at all the place known to-day as Redpath, Redpeth or the Peth.

The Cockplay Plantation.

A third " camp " is marked on the Ordnance Survey in the Cockplay Plantation, and has been mentioned at Institute Meetings and other times. It is also not far from the Villain's Bog. There is said to have been a cockpit in the Cockplay Plantation. Mr. Walter Hedley is our authority. Was the cockpit the " camp "?

Boggle Hole Well.

" There must have been a boggle in Saugh House Park, for there's Boggle Hole Well."—Miss Emily Charlton.

Nanny the Monkey.

" If you go [past Stanton Old House and Beacon Hill] across the moor, on the main turnpike you'll come to a house called Nanny the Monkey. My father knew her; she had a small beer and whisky shop; she had had a monkey." [1] —Mr. Isaac Perceval.

[1] The Misses Adamson of Kirkhill tell me that Nanny the Monkey is a one-storied cottage, on the road from Morpeth to Longhorsley, north of Fenstanton. It is marked on the Ordnance Survey map as Moor-ridge Cottage.

CHAPTER XXV

THE WEAVING INDUSTRY AND DOUBLE NAMES

The Bleaching Green, or the Bleach Green, is the name given by the older people to a little wood at Cambo, south of the blacksmith's shop and of the Two Queens' vegetable garden.

" That would no doubt be where they bleached their webs, but it was before my time."—Mrs. Thomas Hepple.

Others say that any place where washing was dried was called the Bleaching Green.

" *The Knocking Stone,*" *Hartington,* described in Chapter IV, p. 40, " where they used to beat the web."

Hodgson calls it the " battling stone, from its being used to beat or battle the lie out of webs upon, in the bleaching season."

" *Linnlaw Crags* " is marked on the Ordnance Survey.

Miss Mary Murray called it Lint Law, and explained that it is said that the " housewives of Rothley used to bleach their linen or lint there." There is a field also known as Lint Law. The crag and field are close to Rothley Village.

Double Names.

Manside Camp or *Gunners Box,* has been discussed amongst monuments, Chapter XXI, pp. 143-144.

Rugley Walls or Bent House.

" My husband used to tell me that his fore-elders said it was named Rugley Walls because the walls were so rugged; it's the right name on all the old papers about the farm."— Mrs. Thomas Hepple.

Almost everybody else calls the farm " the Bent House "; the site of a cottage and garden, in a field behind, called " Black Benty," has been described on pp. 54 and 117. " Benty," or " Black Benty," is generally understood to be named from the black thatch the cottage had, though it has also been suggested that Bent House means the same as

Rugley Walls.[1]   Both names are far older than the present
house, which is said to have been rebuilt about 1880, and has
over the door the initials

C.E.T.

1882.

" ' Rugley Walls ' is the right name.   Bent House was the
house where the old woman used to live—yes, Black Benty.
Rugley Walls was a terrible rough built place at one time."—
Mr. James Wilkinson.   He was born at Hartington, only a
mile from Rugley Walls.

Kirkheaton is the name on the Ordnance Survey map of
a colliery, just outside our district, which is known to us as
Bog Hall.

" *Shiel Hill*," a farm just outside our district, is thus marked
on Ordnance Survey and other maps, but is known locally as
Shilla Hill.   Hodgson spells it Shillaw-hill.[2]   The present
pronunciation is Shillahill.—Mr. Gilbert Telfer drew attention
to this.

The Holy Burn, or the Willy Burn, or the Holly Burn Lonnin.[3]

Mrs. Trevelyan has remarked on the variations of this name.
She says it is only the old people who call it the Holy Burn,
and that all the young ones call it the Willy Burn.

Two of the older men have been consulted:—Mr. George
Charlton says he has known it by both names all his life;
Mr. James Wilkinson, who lives near it, says it is simply a
matter of pronunciation—the two names Holy Burn and
Willy Burn are one.   " Holy Burn " pronounced in broad
Northumbrian can sound like Hwilly Burn, and therefore
easily becomes Willy Burn.   Is not this an instance of the
way names change in the course of centuries when the
original meaning is lost sight of?   There is a Holy Well just
to the south of the lane, it has been mentioned by Mr.
Wilkinson, and is so marked on the Ordnance Survey, but
to the present generation Willy Burn, or Holly Burn, are
more probable sounding names.   Willows are often called
willies.   Miss McCracken says there used to be beautiful
willows there.   There is no sign of hollies.

---

[1] Bent is a long coarse grass, which was used for thatching.
[2] Hodgson, II, I, p. 277.
[3] A stream is called a " burn " in Northumberland.   A " lonnin " is
a lane.

CHAPTER XXVI

NAMES OF FIELDS

Toothill or Totehill.

There is a field of this name on the Kirkhill farm. Mr. Robert Hepple's family lived there over one hundred years ago, before coming to Rugley Walls. At an Institute Meeting he said that Toothill means Kirk Hill, and reminded us that there is a Toothill at Cambo also, in the field to the east of the present Church, and west of the supposed site of the old chapel, though in the present map of the letting of Cambo grass parks it is called Foot Hill.

Mr. J. Adamson, who farms Kirkhill, took us to see Toothill. It is to the north-east of High Hartington. The hill is small, high and rounded, differing in formation from the surrounding country. It has been made into terraces by the plough in past ages,—by oxen apparently, but the terraces or ridges do not merely run along the sides of the hill, but go right over the top, and the steeper the hill the deeper the ridges. Mr. Adamson, like Mr. Hepple, connects the meaning of Toothill and Kirkhill though it is a couple of fields from the known site of Kirkhill chapel.

> Kirkhill,
> *September 21st, 1922.*

Dear Miss Bosanquet,

You are welcome to put in your book what you have said about the " Toothill " or " Totehill " (Foot Hill is a mistake), or as it was always called, " Tuthill."

I was always under the impression that " Toothill " referred to Chapel Hill or Church Hill, however the late Mr. Fitch used to argue that " Toothill " had nothing to do with Church or Chapel Hill.

173

A curious coincidence occurred about thirty-five or more years ago. I had some fine fat cattle grazing on my " Toot-hill " and five of them died in less than a week, all from Anthrax. The same year or the year after, the Toothill at Cambo was visited by this terrible complaint and the local idea was that being Church hills burial places were there and that worms in course of years had worked up the Anthrax germs from the dead bodies to the surface and cattle had got the disease from that. So much of this is true; Anthrax germs are known in time to be brought from a considerable depth by the action of worms, and Mr. Gow ordered a portion of this field to be railed off after my loss, and it remains so to this day, and cattle don't go there now. The burial place railed off was not supposed to be a human burial ground but the burial ground for dead animals, in fact our losses which occur now and again and are buried.

We heard a good deal of the Toothills in those days when we were having our losses.

Yours sincerely,

J. ADAMSON.

After writing the above I have looked out the word " Toot " in a dictionary. You will find it means to pry or peep about, to be prominent, anything projecting, therefore this may be the hill or a building or anything else.[1]

Mrs. Pearson has always known the Cambo field as Toot-hill, but seeing it spelt as Foot Hill, on the map of the letting of the grass parks, she thought that F must be right, and that Toot was the same word, " just as we say toots for our feet."

There seems little doubt that Mr. Fitch, with his scholarly mind, was correct in saying that the derivation of the word Toothill had nothing to do with Church or Chapel. Much has been written about the derivation of Tuthill, Tote-hill, Toot-hill or Tout-hill, names which occur in many places. A " look out " hill must have been needed in or near all our villages and towns; so also was a church or a chapel and a burial ground.

[1] Heslop, " Northumberland Words," pp. 738, 750, gives a similar definition, and also " Toot, to look out. Tooting-hole, a spy-hole or loophole."

Chapel Hill.

Mr. Henry Codling always said the Chapel had been in that field.[1]—Mr. Edward Keith.

The Cottagers' Field at Cambo has been mentioned in Chapter II, p. 25.

At Rothley there were three fields which were called " the poor folks land." [2]—Mr. James Thornton.

Broad Rigs at Rothley.

" The rigs are broad."—Mr. James Thornton.

The Leazes. The Bought Lease.

In an eighteenth century map at Wallington a field is marked " the bought lease."—Mr. G. M. Trevelyan.

There are still two fields next each other in the same part of the estate, close to Wallington on the north, which are called " the horse leazes " and " the cow leazes," Mr. W. Hedley says. He knows the word " bought," as used in the hills, for the places where they milk the ewes, and Burns uses the word with that meaning.

Mr. Edward Keith points out that Leazes is a common name in Northumberland for pastures, derived probably from the Saxon " laeswi," a pasture. Fields, called by this name, are generally near the house, and this one would have been " within sight and control of the old Tower."

The vowel sound in " bought " is pronounced like " ou " in " bough," so also in Northumbrian is the word " bought," meaning purchased. Mrs. Trevelyan suggested that this field had been bought.

Brocket, and also Heslop, quoting Dr. Murray's " New English Dictionary," give " bought " as a " sheepfold." " It is specially a pen for confining ewes at milking time." " Leazes " are defined by Heslop as " stinted grass pastures . . . reserved for hay at stated times each year."

---

[1] Hodgson, II, I, p. 286. " . . . Tote-hill; and the western part of the field in which the Chapel of Cambo stood is called by that name." The field must have been divided and the wood planted since his time. The field to the west of the wood is called Toot Hill; that to the east of the wood is called Chapel Hill.

[2] It was implied that it would be there they grazed their cows; the subject under discussion was the simple life in the old days, and how they managed on the low wages—8d. a day for a mason—when Oakford Bridge was built in the eighteenth century.

High Leazes and *Low Leazes* are fields to the north of Rothley Village.—Miss Mary Murray.

Blackcock is the name of another field close to Rothley Crag House, but the name is less used now.—Miss Mary Murray.

Fields on Rugley Walls Farm.

" Poor Robin " is said to be so-called from the flower that grows there.[1]—Mrs. Thomas Hepple.

Cobbler's Rigs.

" My father used to say there had been, or there must have been, a cobbler there once."—Mr. Robert Hepple.

Field on Donkin Ridge Farm.

" Hungry Hill " is so named " being a bare field."—Miss Bessie Anderson, Close House.   She lived as a child at Rothley near the field.

Tommy's Island has been mentioned, in Chapter XIV, p. 110, by Mr. Isaac Perceval as " a little wood with a bit of a bog across it," where he found a spirit still.

" Tommy —— had two horses in poor condition, and very weak, and they plewed [2] there for a considerable time, and after that it got [3] ' Tommy's Island ' "—Mr. Isaac Perceval.

The Pit Field.

About three years ago a beast [4] was missing from a field closely adjoining Cambo, and inquiry and search for it proved fruitless.   Several weeks after, Miss Nixon was walking across the field in question when the sound of running water close by arrested her attention.   On stopping and looking around she discovered a hole yawning at her feet.   This, naturally, alarmed her very much, as another step on her part would have had the inevitable result.   She at once ran and told

---

[1] This we understood to be the same as Ragged Robin.
[2] Ploughed.
[3] That is, it got the name of.
[4] One of the young cattle.

her father, who happened to be near, and on his coming, with others who quickly gathered up, it was discovered that the hole was a pit shaft. It was well made, the sides being built up with bricks, and it would be upwards of sixty feet deep, as near as one could guess, and there was water running with considerable force in the bottom. There was cattle hair and there were marks round the mouth of the hole which plainly showed the fate of the missing beast.

It could be seen that beams of wood had been placed over the mouth of the pit shaft when it had ceased to be worked and in the course of many years the wood had rotted. The beast would be probably galloping from the flies, as it was summer time and the weather was hot; the general opinion was that the wood had given way with its weight. Bags of shavings were lighted and lowered down but they would not burn at a certain distance, which proved that the air was bad. The dim outline of the beast could be seen at the bottom. If a stone were thrown down it was several seconds before it reached the bottom, and when it did so it made a hollow booming sound.

The field is called the " Pit Field." My father, who is shepherd, has walked through it hundreds of times without any mishap, although there are signs of several pit shafts in other parts of the field.—Written by Miss Hilda Hedley.

Mrs. Trevelyan adds: " This pit is supposed not to have been worked for at least one hundred years." [1]

There are heaps of earth overgrown with grass, where refuse from the pits have been thrown.

[1] See Hodgson, II, I, p. 276.

CHAPTER XXVII

NAMES OF ROADS, AND POINTS ON ROADS

MOST of the " road " names have already been mentioned.

The " *New Line*,"—the " new " coaching road between Belsay and Otterburn made about 1840.

" *The Kil' Lonnin*,"—the lane turning off towards the lime kilns which there used to be to the west of the road from Cambo to Harwood Gate. It turns off just beyond Cambo school.—Mr. James Wilkinson.

" *The Church Track* " from Rothley to Kirkwhelpington, across the corner of Rugley Walls garden, and in front of Elf Hills Farm.—Mr. Robert Hepple.

Somebody else has mentioned that it leaves the main road from Scots Gap to Rothbury at the stile by Oakford Bridge.

" The Church Track " is an old road, not a driving road to-day. We use the word " road " here meaning way, whether it be driving road, bridle road, or footpath.

Lady Blackett's Drive and the Coach Turns.

Lady Blackett's Drive, a grassy road, runs from Rothley Village, through the fields, to a point on the road between Harwood Gate and Long Witton, which is known as the Coach Turns. It is said that in the eighteenth century, Lady Blackett, wife of Sir Walter Blackett, used to drive up that way to the then new Rothley Castle.

There used to be a wide turn where the drive joins the main road, but it is now partly enclosed, and the little Rothley Church stands on part of the Coach Turns.

Miss Mary Murray and others at an Institute Meeting thought the coach, which turned there, was the Wallington one.

Miss Barbara Blain, who first mentioned the Coach Turns,

had heard of it from Miss Aynsley of Long Witton, and Miss Aynsley believed that a public coach ran along the main road, passing the Coach Turns and Long Witton.[1]

Hawkers used to light fires and spend the night at the Coach Turns.

Salters Nick.[2]

" Mr. Codling of Hartburn told me that the smugglers of salt used to stay there during the day, hiding their ponies in the cleft of the rocks, which is difficult to find, on the Angerton part of Shaftoe Crag. The excise officials knew they were there, but never molested them, they were such dangerous persons."—Mr. Edward Keith.

The Pant or Pan Gate, is the gate leading off the Cambo to Scots Gap road in the direction of Saugh House.

Nowadays, it is sometimes called the Pan Gate, but Mrs. Pearson says we always called it the Pant Gate.

" Mr. Nixon said there must have been a pant there." [3]— Miss McCracken.

Steng Cross, Winter's Gibbet [4] or the Stob.

Steng Cross is the name on maps, and the foundation of the old cross is still to be seen near the Gibbet; but none of us dream of calling the place anything but " the Gibbet," or the " Stob," which means the same thing.

" The Stob heft," [5] was the flock of sheep on the part of the farm, on the moor, near the Gibbet.—Miss McCracken.

" *Billy's Bank*," a hill on the way from Rugley Walls to Cambo on the old coaching road, is said to be called after the great-uncle of the late Mr. Thomas Hepple. " He used

[1] Possibly both statements are correct. I think I once saw in an old road book that a coach ran along that road and that one of the stages was " Rothley Shiel."

Mr. Walter Hedley knows that " the coach horses—the Wallington coach horses "—ran in the field at Wallington called " the Barn Flat."

[2] It is on the so-called " Salters Road."

[3] Heslop defines " pant " as " a public water fountain."

[4] Chapter XXIII, p. 162. Steng or stang means a wooden post.

[5] I understand from Mr. W. Hedley that the " heft " is not the flock of sheep, but the part of the farm on which that particular flock is pastured. There may be several hefts on a hill farm, each with its flock, and the sheep know their own heft.

to help them up with their loads with an old horse." [1]—Mrs. Thomas Hepple.

"*Big Robin's Bank*" and "*Little Robin's Bank*" are between Rothley and the Lakes.—Miss Bessie Anderson.

Harwood Gate.

This name is given now to two houses where three roads meet; the old coaching road from Newcastle to Jedburgh turns west to Elsdon, and a road turns east to Morpeth.

A few yards west of the present Harwood Gate there was once a public-house and a toll gate where "travellers had to pay to get through"; it used to be very busy at one time. There is a garden by itself, marking the place where the public-house and toll gate used to be. The reason why so many people used to gather up there was that there were tilesheds, close by at Gallowshill, where there is a plantation; they made drain pipes for draining the fields; it was the time when so much draining was being done; and the lime kil' between Hartington and Gallowshill was working; and these employed a great many men. Droves of cattle used to be driven past, and there were carriers' carts, and farmers' carts. These facts were given by Miss L. Davison and her family. The older generation have lived at Harwood Gate a great many years, perhaps fifty years, and have heard the talk of old people who lived there before them. From them they know what carryings on there once were in this now lonely spot.

The Shop Trees is still the name for four trees by the same roadside but a mile or two farther west.

"In pre-railway days, when great droves of cattle were driven over the Carter into these northern counties, it was usual to have them shod with plates of iron, to prevent the animals falling lame when travelling great distances over rough, gritty turnpike roads. Up to about eighty years ago a flourishing blacksmith's business—employing from three to four men—was carried on right up on the Harwood moors, about a mile from Winter's Gibbet, on the Elsdon road. As the Chevy Chase coaches and lines of carriers' carts used this

---

[1] This must have been "Mr. William Hepple, farmer at Rugley Walls, who is near ninety years old," who gave Hodgson the story of the fairies.—Hodgson, II, I, p. 309.

road between Jedburgh and Newcastle, up to the building of the new road between Belsay and Otterburn, the shoeing business must have been a heavy item; but it is no less a fact that this shoeing of cattle was the leading line in the business. Transit by rail has made this operation a thing of the past, and almost forgotten by the third generation of those who practised it. In the place of the noise and bustle of the old moorland smithy, nothing now remains but a lonely, wind-swept clump of trees by the roadside."—Written by Mr. Edward Keith.

Mr. Davison of Harwood Gate and Mr. Davison of Low Fairnley confirmed the fact that " the Shop Trees " mark the site of the old blacksmith's shop, where the coach horses were shod, between Harwood Gate and the Gibbet.

Mr. Charlton said " the farmers from about here used to go up to Falkirk Fair to get their Kyloes,[1] and Mrs. Hall of Scots Gap's brother—a Hedley—was one of those who used to be engaged to go and drive them down. And I've heard them say that in still older days they used to plate them."

Mr. R. Adam Wilson said cattle certainly were shod when they went lame: " I have butched three that were shod." The shoe was in two parts so that the hoof could divide, otherwise they could not have walked. There were three brothers, Scotchmen from Whitelees, near Carter Bar, who drove the cattle from Falkirk past Clock Mill, and when Mr. Wilson was quite a lad, only sixteen, he had the buying from them for his uncle. When he was only seven years old he was herding sheep. He added that the Canadian cattle, which had been used for ploughing, were shod when they came over.

Mr. William Wilson has one of the old shoes.

---

[1] Kyloes are small, shaggy Highland cattle.

APPENDIX A

" THERE is a curious link between Cambo and Fenstanton "—
of which Cambo was unaware until after the prizes[1] had been
awarded—" Capability Brown, who was born at Kirkharle
and educated at Cambo School, in later life owned the Manor
of Fenstanton in Huntingdonshire, and is buried in the church
there. Miss Peet lives in the house he used to live in. She
has in her possession a large portfolio of his maps, dated 1777,
showing the fields with their names, most of which have now
gone out of use. The maps are very much like the map which
was made for Sir Walter Blackett, which now hangs in the gun-
room at Wallington, and was probably done by the same
hand, either Capability Brown or his secretary."—Written by
Mrs. Charles Trevelyan, June 2nd, 1923.

The Fenstanton Burial Register gives:—

" 1782 Brown, Lancelot, Lord of this Manor, Feb. 16th.

1786 Brown, Bridget, widow of Lancelot, Lord of this
Manor, Sept. 3rd.

1792 Brown, Mrs., wife of Lancelot, Lord of this Manor,
Dec. 9th.

1801 Brown, Lancelot, Lord of this Manor, March 7th.

1808 Brown, John, Admiral and Lord of this Manor,
May 14th."

There is a tomb to Capability Brown (the first Lancelot)
and his family in Fenstanton Church, showing that the
second Lancelot, who was an M.P., and John were his sons,
and giving the following verse:

[1] Preface, p. 5.

Ye Sons of Elegance, who truly taste,
  The simple charms that genuine art supplies,
Come from the sylvan scenes this genius graced,
  And offer here your tributary sighs.
But know that more than genius slumbers here,
  Virtues were his which art's best power transcend,
Come ye superior train, who these revere,
  And weep the Christian, Husband, Father, Friend.

—Supplied by Miss Peet.

In later life Sir George Trevelyan was convinced that Capability Brown had designed the Wallington gardens and Garden House. Mr. Edward Keith pointed out to Sir George that there is a marked resemblance between them and the gardens and house at Claremont in Surrey, which it is known that Capability Brown designed at about the same date that the Wallington gardens were made. The date on the lead spouting on Wallington Garden House is 1766. (Compare Chapter III, p. 36.)

APPENDIX B

TWO TOASTS

Here's to the Rainbow, bonny, red and green,
Here's to the laddie I often seen,
Health to his body, money to his purse,
And heaven when he dies, I wish him no worse.

Here's to cold winter, likewise cold frost,
I toss up again for the lad I have lost,
May he ever live single and ever live free,
And tied to another I never shall be.

—Written down by Miss L. Davison.

APPENDIX C

Here's two Dukes just come from Spain,
To ask the loan of your daughter Jane.
My daughter Jane is far too young,
She cannot bear your prattling tongue,
The naughty girl she won't come out,
She won't come out, she won't come out,
The naughty girl she won't come out,
    To help the ladies dancing.

The pretty girl she has come out,
She has come out, she has come out,
The pretty girl she has come out,
    To help the ladies dancing.

—Written down by the late Mrs. Robert Davison, Cambo.

This is another version of the song given in Chapter XX,
p. 133. Mrs. Davison also wrote down her version of " In
and out the Windows," p. 132, giving two extra verses:

Now they are married, now they are married,
Now they are married, as you have done before.

Now they are parted, now they are parted,
Now they are parted, as you have done before.

APPENDIX D

CHILDHOOD AT HOLLINGSIDE, 1853-1865

OLD George Skelton was our occasional gardener. I was once talking to him, when a toad appeared, and I was going to pick it up, but he said: " Eh, Missy, divn't touch yon, it'll poison ye! " It is perhaps worth while to record this, as being a survival of the old superstition that toads are poisonous. Childy Wynd, you know, changed his wicked stepmother to a venom-spitting toad! Apropos of superstitions, we were once jumping off the nursery table, over the head of a child standing beside it, when that amusement was stopped by the nurse, because the jumped-over child would never grow! Our nails were never cut on Friday nor would anyone, if they could help it, begin anything on that day. I remember, too, when one of my first teeth came out, it was thrown into the fire with a pinch of salt and the appropriate rhyme requesting it to come again. Owing to early training, I never, after eating an egg, omit to make a hole in the shell " so that the witches may not sail over the sea in it! " Once some squirrels began to frequent " the little wood " and Henderson shot them, to my mother's great annoyance, because he thought them unlucky.

For a north-country woman, my mother, who was by way of being strong-minded, was not superstitious, but she could not altogether escape the consequences of her Northumbrian breeding, and she habitually practised one charm, at least. She, and her sister too, used, in Spring, to look for a four-leaved clover, and keep it in her purse for the rest of the year as a luck-bringer.

" Old Bella Young," my mother's monthly nurse, practised many rites pertaining to her craft, such as " stepping up " a baby before it left the room of its birth, so that it might be sure to rise in life; not washing the palms of its hands,

so that it might become rich; and refraining from cutting its
nails lest it should steal.—Written by Mrs. Apperley, County
Durham, a relation of our member, Mrs. Carr-Ellison.
Hollingside is near Durham, but Mrs. Apperley belongs to a
Northumbrian family.

Miss E. Charlton, Cambo, supplies the rhyme used when
burning first teeth,—" We always said it":—

> Fire, fire, burn a tooth,
> God send me my tooth again,
> Not a black one but a white one,
> Not a crook'd one but a straight one.

APPENDIX E

WHEN playing ball, the number of times one could catch without a break was thus counted by our Border maid-servants, which reminds one of old shepherds' scoring.

> One-ry, two-ery, tikery, seven,
> Allabo, attabo, ten or eleven,
> Pin pan, paskidan,
> Twiddle-um, tweddle-um, twenty-wan.

—Mrs. Sisson, a friend of our member Mrs. Carr-Ellison; Mrs. Sisson used to live at Pallinsburn in another part of Northumberland.

APPENDIX F

THE following extracts are from a letter, written with her own hand, by Mrs. Haldane, the mother of Lord Haldane, formerly Lord Chancellor. She was a Burdon Sanderson. Born on April 9th, 1825, she died on May 20th, 1925. She used to live at Otterburn Dene.

CLOAN, AUCHTERARDER, N.B.
June 9th, 1923.

DEAR MRS. TREVELYAN,

. . . I have a very vivid recollection of the Inn at Cambo, when I first knew it, at about three years of age.

My father was at that time a keen sportsman, and I think the meet of the Northumbrian hounds must have been there or very near. . . . I cannot remember any signboard over the door, which opened on to a broad, cobble-stoned platform on which a carriage and four could be easily turned. Beyond this space and opposite to the Hotel, was a well-filled kitchen garden, very attractive to us small children. . . . The garden gate was nearly opposite to the front door of the Hotel. . . . I think there was a slight rise up to the platform (may I call it) of the Hotel from the coaching road, but my impression of Cambo is that of being on the crown of a hill. My mother went on to Wallington to see your dear ancestress who was then advanced in life—Lady Trevelyan—leaving us to return for her. My remembrance was of a beautiful museum belonging to Lady Trevelyan, which my mother described and we longed to see, but my mother thought there might be a disturbance or fatigue to Lady Trevelyan. Elizabeth has told you of our admiration of Miss Julia Trevelyan and her horse.

189

To return to Cambo.   I think the greater part of the village was occupied by stabling, and houses for employées, and kennels, but beyond them there was a tempting shop where everything we could wish for could be purchased—a delightful attraction for us.

As to the road from Otterburn and Elsdon it was very dreary. After passing Cambo the roadside trees were small, then it crossed one of the most desolate moors I can remember, of which I can only now make comparison by the surroundings of the Escurial in Spain, and round about Madrid. . . . On this moor not far from the road was erected a gibbet, on which was hung an effigy of the murderer of the old woman, in sight of her cottage. The chains rattled with the wind audibly as we passed along, and the story was not lost in telling in our nursery. . . . The road must have been eventually altered as there was a deep excavation at Raylees, which must have occurred during 1835 or 6; in the winter of 1837 we passed that way, posting through deep snow in a cutting made not long before for the road. It was changed so far and turned from Elsdon because, I suppose . . . there was a very steep hill to encounter, ruinous to horses, before reaching the dreary moor. My mother, infant sister and we had obstinate attacks of whooping cough, and were ordered to leave Otterburn Dene for a warmer climate. We were packed into the family carriage, with two pairs of horses, a most uncomfortable experience, as we little girls had to stand during the journey.

A dentist—Mr. Nightingale—used to come out from Newcastle to the inn at Cambo, and Miss Haldane wrote in 1923 of how her mother drove over to see him one winter's day in an open dogcart. " You drove up and she remembers the ponies' feet on the cobbles (they drove four ponies very often), and the feeling of hunger . . . and there were pictures of pheasants on the walls. They always had chops and plain pudding for dinner . . . and the children were sometimes allowed to go and pick blackcurrants in the nice little garden. There was no gentleman's house, but a charming shop where one bought whips and patches for dolls' dresses. The dentist hurt her very badly and she says she will never forget the drive back again in the cold and rain, with her aching tooth, past the Gibbet; the clanking chains frightened her terribly. It was the year Lord Eldon died and her father was much away with Lord Eldon during his last illness, and the girls were left in charge of a governess. . . .

They used to enjoy seeing the beautiful beeches at Wallington after the bare country near the Gibbet, with only stunted trees and no corn or houses. Miss Julia Trevelyan was about Mrs. Haldane's mother's age, and was an unusual lady, for she didn't marry but rode about on a white horse doing good. . . .

It used to be a great treat to go over to Elsdon fair and buy gingerbread, which was made in the form of little men. Small tables loaded with thick gingerbread in squares were set out on the green. . . . The old coachman drove four ponies across the moor; there was no road from Elsdon to Otterburn Dene (formerly Davyshiel).

The cottage people lived in ' but and ben,' the former for the males, the latter for the females; they ate out of a big bowl each with a spoon, and barley scones were always baked.

She remembers the coaches that used to come past Otterburn. The Chevy Chase brought the news of the passing of the Reform Bill in 1832, and her father got all the family and the household out to the front of the house to wait for the coach's arrival, to be first to hear the news."

---

[1] The outer and inner room of a two-roomed house. Compare the expressions " by-out " and " by-in," or " out-by " and " in-by."—Brocket.

INDEX OF CONTRIBUTORS

INDEX OF AUTHORITIES AND OTHER PERSONS

196

PRINTED IN GREAT BRITAIN BY
NORTHUMBERLAND PRESS LIMITED, NEWCASTLE-UPON TYNE